The Mind Behind Wealth

The Real Guide To Your Financial Success

Verses Kindler Publication.

Verses Kindler Publication.
Website: www.verseskindlerpublication.com

The Mind Behind Wealth

The Real Guide To Your Financial Success

By: Mrs. Komal Auti

ISBN: 978-93-5605-488-2

SELF-HELP STORIES 1st Edition
Price: INR 499/$22

Disclaimer

"The Mind Behind Wealth: The Real Guide to Your Financial Success" is an original work by Komal Auti. The author has strived to ensure the content is free from plagiarism.

The characters and events depicted in this book may be fictional or inspired by real-life experiences. However, they are not intended to cause offense or to represent any particular caste, system, or individual. Any similarity to actual persons, places, or institutions is purely coincidental and unintentional.

The author assumes full responsibility for any instances of plagiarism that may be found within this work. The publisher is not liable for any such instances.

Acknowledgement

To My Readers,

This book is my heartfelt offering to all of you. I have been coaching people in finance for over a decade and half, helping them make decisions to have a stable future. Yet I had always wanted to reach the many whom I could not personally coach. This book is my attempt to extend that reach and share practical insights, tools, and strategies that we discuss in our sessions. For the last two years, this project had been waiting patiently, tucked away amid life's demands. It was only in the last eight months, while I was at home recovering from cancer, that I found the time, energy, and determination to complete it. These months have just been rollercoaster emotions—moments of reflection, resilience, and ultimately, renewal of purpose.

A Journey Through Life's Ups and Downs

Life has been a mixed bag of blessings and trials. The younger years were blissful, filled with dreams and possibilities. When I met my husband, my life began to find direction and meaning. Together, we faced struggles and celebrated victories. Just when everything seemed stable, life threw another curveball in the way of my diagnosis with cancer.

The last few months are an example of how life is unpredictable. But the challenge is that it only provides opportunities in disguise. It puts strength to the test and pushes us to rise above it all. To those who suffer difficulties, I say: be resilient. Problems are bound to arise, but so are our powers to overcome them and be stronger.

Gratitude to My Pillars of Support

This book would not be possible without a great number of people who stood by me throughout.

To my family and friends, thank you for being my anchor. My professional colleagues and the Team DK Mission Force, your dedication and belief in me have been inspiring. A heartfelt thank you to the editors and publishers, whose expertise and patience have brought this book to life.

Special Thanks to My Husband, Mr. Dilip Auti

Deepest gratitude to my husband, Dilip; a man who has been a true international business coach and strategist. His wisdom and insights into understanding the management of the international business environment have offered me invaluable guidance. In many late-night discussions and also through moments of doubt, your encouragement has allowed me to continue. Your belief in this book and in me is a testament to your strength and love.

This book is as much yours as it is mine, a testament to your influence and our shared resilience.

To all of you, my readers, thanks. It is for you that this book exists, and I hope it serves as a source of knowledge, inspiration, and empowerment.

With immense gratitude,
Komal Auti

Table of Contents

Chapter 1: The Power of Mindset

Raghav, a reticent school teacher, had always assumed that just enough to get by would be all he needed. Virtue was contentment, he reminded himself. His cousin Arjun had built for himself a life, however, which made Raghav think otherwise. We become what we think about. If you think small, you stay small. It's not greed to want more; it's growth. This conversation made Raghav realize that he had been limiting his ambitions and hence was not growing to the best of his ability. Inspired, he shifted his mindset that aspiring for more opens doors for greater opportunities. *Zindagi mein bas utna hi chahiye jitna zaroori ho.*

Money is not something we possess, make, spend, save, or invest; it is quite closely linked with the mindset of how we think about it, how we perceive it, and what makes up our lives. As I write about my journey in understanding the mind's relationship with financial success, something has crystallized: prosperity begins in the mind. It is the most powerful tool we have at our disposal to shape our financial futures, but, in a country like India, most people unwittingly hold themselves back financially through poor beliefs about money. Let's explore how this mindset often forms the shadow between where we are and where we could be. *Mujhe pakka pata hai, yeh kitab aapka nazariya badal degi.*

When viewed from a larger view, Indians have a rather special relationship with money. Our history has several eras of significant wealth and economic might; however, along the passage of time, people's perceptions towards money have evolved, mostly with mistrust. Many think that people have a large amount of wealth due to greedy dispositions and that people who are successful are somehow favored. Such misconceptions shape our mindset of creating money and viewing who holds it. It limits us from being who we ought to be and makes us stagnant instead.

How the Mind Connects with Financial Success

The mind is where the journey of finances begins. If you believe that money is hard to earn, then it will be so, as long as you exist and live your life in such a way and as long as you portray such a situation around you. However, people who hold a belief that money is the means to further growth and abundance mostly find themselves in greater successful financial positions.

I have sat with hundreds of people who simply believed that wealth happened to a few select individuals, that opportunities to create prosperity were few and far between, or that they, somehow, did not deserve to have wealth. But in each case, I've come to understand that those beliefs create a self-fulfilling prophecy. If one keeps simply telling himself that money is inaccessible to him, then, of course, it will be. A mind creates much power to shape not only our emotional state of being but also our financial reality, whereby building a mindset that believes in abundance can give us permission to go after wealth fully and openly with the utmost confidence.

I understand a change and noticed that when someone transforms their thinking around money from fear into possibility, the opportunities tend to multiply. This is not some mystic concept; it's a realistic observation. Those who are open to wealth, see the world the right way about money, and believe that it is feasible that their financial goals could be realized seem to do things that would, in fact, push them towards becoming wealthy.

Historical and Regional Attitudes Toward Wealth in India

India was the land of spices, textiles, and precious stones. It attracted trade from various parts of the world. We have the backbone of our prosperity during the Gupta and Mughal empires, with well-established trade routes and an economy doing very well. However, the British era has drastically changed the economics of our land. Resources were drained, industries dismantled, and once-flowing streams of wealth cut off. This transformation from prosperity to poverty over the course of time instilled deep caution in the Indian psyche towards wealth. As a society, we began to look askance at wealth. In traditional Indian culture, particularly with respect to the beliefs supported in religions and philosophies, the emphasis often is on asceticism and minimalism. Detachment from material wealth is growing, and much of the pursuit of money is seen as against spiritual growth.

I have seen people, especially in rural areas, criticize those people who have a lot of wealth. A behind-the-scenes notion seems to exist regarding the fact that a person with money more than his or her needs did something wrong to acquire it. This particular cultural context against wealth might overshadow an individual's motivation towards monetary success. However, in other areas, there is a different view toward wealth. *Aapka is mein kya khayal hai?*

Some of the states like Gujarat and Maharashtra have good entrepreneurial and commercial leadership. Business acumen is appreciated and treated for developing wealth, as it is part of mainstream activity. The fact is that among the communities of Marwaris and Parsis, entrepreneurship is very popular. I have come to realize people from such communities perceive money in a much healthier perspective as they grew up perceiving that it is used for growth and not to shying away from it. Such regional disparity shows that it requires the proper cultivation of the perception of money.

The Common Indian Mindset

As a matter of fact, India has very deep historical roots regarding the association of wealth and prosperity. This has been due to its different cultures, religions, and social structures. The Indian people have wonderfully and efficiently coped with a changing economic vision while retaining unique insights into what money is all about. The attitude toward money in India is not monolithic or negative, to say the least. *Voh kehte hai na, sabka apna alag tareeka hai yahan par.*

India's cultural heritage has always been one of moderation but it has also had a profound sense of contentment, and this was based on ancient precepts of spirituality, such as those laid down in the Bhagavad Gita. We Indians, see attachment to material possessions as something to be renounced and instead focus on seeking inner peace. While this sometimes gets misconstrued as a lack of ambition, it's critical to understand the sense of this approach. For centuries, Indians had been practicing living within their means and contentment with what they already had, not being obsessed with material wealth to an unhealthy degree. It helped provide stability and enabled families to stick through thick and thin financially.

Modern India, however, has seen a huge change in general orientation since the 1990s, especially in the era of liberalization of the economy. Globalisation, penetration of technology, and skyrocketing aspirations of young Indians have changed the very approach to the concept of wealth and the pursuit of it. Such faith is growing that one can actually generate power in creating wealth. Start-ups are growing, a healthy middle class has emerged, and values have begun to shift. Young entrepreneurs continue to emerge on the horizon in the cities of Bengaluru, Hyderabad, and Mumbai with new avenues to explore and redefine success. *Har ghar mein aaj hume ek jalta chirag dekhne milta hai.*

A part of India's change of mindset is to want to put traditionalism together with innovation. A large proportion of the young Indians today wish to acquire wealth not simply to feather their own nests but for the benefit of their families, to build up their communities, and to contribute back to society. This is a desirable attitude whereby money is viewed as a means towards the betterment of one's person in terms of both personal and social ends rather than an end in itself. Dharma remains a very central factor in shaping financial objectives. The many successful entrepreneurs and business leaders of India speak to the prioritizing of ethics and community in the pursuit of wealth, making it manifestly possible to thrive in a very competitive environment without losing the middle ground.

The younger generation of India increasingly breaks away from a more normative path that are government jobs or inherited family businesses to innovation, risk-taking, and entrepreneurial ventures.

This new mindset is particularly noteworthy because of the role education plays in it. With increased access to education and exposure to worldwide interaction, there is more belief in the creation of wealth rather than inheritance alone. It is a big change in collective psyche as young Indians are now aware of their ability to shape up their financial destiny.

Social frameworks that had earlier, 'bound' people's aspirations relating to economic opportunities are changing too. Such as caste-oriented professions or family expectations concerning professional choices have become less binding in modern times. Education, hard work, and ingenuity can today propel someone from a modest background right to the top of the socio-economic scale. This is a long way from the old days when all-important economic futures were bound by family lineage or society's role assignments.

While this is a welcome phenomenon, tremendous traditionalistic thinking still dominates rural India, with financial conservatism continuing to dominate the psyche. However, even here, awareness about the need for financial literacy and savings in the form of investments can be noted. Initiatives such as the Jan Dhan Yojana and digital payment systems by the government continue to increase the participatory ratio of all segments of society in the formal economy.

India's financial mentality also seems to be very advanced. *Humari soch kaafi aage badh chuki hai.* Most Indians fear debt and will not, on principle, permit their money to be put into any kind of pointless financial risk-taking. As prudent as the approach often is, viewed from many angles it can be incredibly successful for long-term stability. Unlike some Western economies - which increase growth with borrowed dollars - Indians generally prefer saving and wise investment of surplus funds; or, to use a phrase with recent history, a rather careful approach that doesn't see security play second fiddle to success.

What has strongly emerged in India's dynamic mindset toward wealth is a fusion of aspiration and responsibility. Many erstwhile undesirable connotations associated with financial success have lost allure, yet there's an understanding that wealth needs to be earned in the right and proper way and used with sincerity. Philanthropy and social impact are now seen as integral to true success. The new financial consciousness holds the opinion that money is not a simple constituent of individual success but rather a good force in the transformation of society. More and more wealth is seen as a means of contributing to positive change in society. This serves as the cornerstone of India's new financial consciousness, spurring its rapid development.

Importance of Taking a Positive Perception of Money

How we view money determines the amount that comes into our lives. My personal life and conversations with people around me suggest that the way of thinking about money gives some sort of mental block to its abundance. People feel awkward talking about money or wanting to be rich or wealthy. Money is just a tool; it depends on what we make out of it.

There are tons of stories about people who after gaining money lost their values. This belief made me live with the chronic anxiety that I never had enough money, but simultaneously, I felt guilty if I wanted to have more. I eventually changed my mind and realized that money neither is good, nor bad, in itself-it just happens to be a neutral medium for increasing one's fulfillment in life and for doing good. It allowed me to realize that positive thinking does not have the implications of parading your selfish greed and immoralities, but about valuing the opportunities money can bring. Wealth doesn't corrupt; it reveals who you already are.

Money manifests not only its own values but also increases the capability to act on sturdy values in a greater proportion. Therefore, it empowers you to donate money to charities, help people in need, or even create jobs for people. This thinking empowered me to earn and manage wealth without feeling guilty. The notion of money among Indians needs to shift from suspicious to empowering.

Prosperity is not just making more money; it's the understanding that financial strength is a guaranteed safety, a sort of guarantee for your future, and thereby ensures to free others from bondage as well. It is all about people's perception of money with guilt or fear appended to it.

Effects of Family and Social Influence on Financial Goals

Aapka mindset aapki life mein bahut bada role play karta hai.
The biggest influence on our financial mindset is our family and social environment. Money is one of the taboo topics within Indian families. Growing up, kids hardly ever heard discussions on creating wealth, investing, or financial planning. Most of any discussion was centred around saving money or just barely getting by on what a person did have. This is not atypical. In Indian households, people's focus is on survival rather than improving one's self.

I have seen that unconscious family environments leave children with limiting beliefs about money. The subconscious memory from day to day of hearing "money doesn't grow on trees" or "we can't afford that" as a child builds a mental framework that limits the potential that could be the reality of the grown-up adult. Perhaps these children grow up in an environment where, no matter how hard one works, there is always a lack of money. So, it's hard to have belief in financial abundance later in life.

In contrast, open discussion on financial planning, investments, and entrepreneurship gives a much healthier attitude towards wealth in children. They learn to view money as a growth resource rather than seeing it as scarce. Indeed, I have realized that stark differences in attitude arise from discussion with people from entrepreneurial backgrounds, where their parents would encourage them to take some level of risk and invest into opportunities with hopes of tangible financial success.

A very important role of social influence is played while defining our mindset related to finance. In society where wealth sometimes is held under suspicion, mediocrity also seeps in easily. If all the people around you think wealth is out of reach and not desirable then it requires great power to break free and chase financial success. On the other hand, if you are surrounded by successful empowered financially activated others, it motivates you to lift your aim.

That is the reason why it is even more crucial to know the people and surroundings we are exposing ourselves to. I have learned that people who promote growth, positive thoughts, and creating wealth have really opened up my wallet and investment books to world-changing things in finance. It's not about cutting oneself totally out of friends or family members whose thoughts might be limiting, but it is a lot about keeping things in balance between living true to one's roots while also embracing a mindset of prosperity.

All I can say is...

Generally speaking, our relationship with money will be very clear if our mindset remains optimistic regarding earning assets. From some pre-conceptions about wealth based on history to notions of what family and society regard as acceptable, all these factors become cemented into our perceptions and pursuit of financial success. In India, where many traditional views about money exist which only create unnecessary barriers, it's imperative first to break free from these limiting beliefs and to develop an abundance mindset.

The power of the mind to generate wealth is not to be underestimated. *Aapka mindset aapki zindagi badal sakta hai.*

We will change not only our own financial futures but perhaps even the future of those around us by thinking positively about money, understanding its potential and utilizing it as a means to pursue personal and societal advancement.

All this begins with changing the way we think and feel about wealth, a shift in mindset that can culminate into a life of more financial freedom, opportunity and fulfilment.

Exercise:

Q1. Write down beliefs you hold about money that may be limiting your potential. Then, challenge that belief by writing down a more empowering alternative.

Example : Money is difficult to earn - Money always flows towards me easily

Belief holding you back	*Challenge that belief*

Q2. The Wealth Mindset Quiz

- Instructions: Answer the following questions to assess your mindset towards money:
    1. I believe that anyone can achieve financial success, regardless of their background. (Agree / Disagree)
    2. Money is a tool for personal growth and societal good. (Agree / Disagree)

3. I feel guilty when I want to make more money. (Agree / Disagree)
4. I view financial risks as opportunities to grow wealth. (Agree / Disagree)
5. I believe that financial success is possible through hard work, knowledge, and creativity. (Agree / Disagree)

Chapter 2: Financial Planning for Success

Monetary success doesn't mean only gaining money but also about how to spend it. Most think that having a lot of income will be sufficient for financial security, which is quite false. One can earn a lot but fall into financial dire straits if proper planning isn't observed. Financial planning is what manages a person's income, savings, expenses, and investments towards a balance that sets one toward long-term financial stability.

In this chapter, we'll be talking about good financial planning being based upon two big ideas: financial psychology and financial philosophy. Sounds like fancy-pants terms, but it's actually pretty simple: understanding how you think about money and how you want to use it. Your mindset about money is the difference between whether you save it, spend it, or invest it.

After all, as they say, "It is hard to achieve financial goals without some planning." One is starting a career or getting old into retirement; a good financial plan comes with it. It sets you up for the various stages of your life: early adulthood, mid-career, and retirement - and also provides a safety net for non-planned events like emergencies and inflation.

Dhan kamana hi kaafi nahi hai. Usse sahi se sambhalna bhi aana chahiye.

So, you will learn how to achieve a healthy relationship with money, formulate realistic financial objectives, and prepare yourself for the various financial persecutions thrown in your way. Financial planning is not a once-forever plan; rather, it is a journey toward a secure and successful life.

Financial Psychology and Philosophy

Introduction to Financial Psychology

Financial psychology is, in simple words, how people think about money and manage it. It involves emotions and habits that determine spending, saving, and investing. For most people, their financial decisions rely on their mindset about money. When people look at money as a means to grow or just as something to be spent. The way we think of money really has a big impact on our financial success.

People are either spenders or savers. While they may both earn the same income, their returns might be worlds apart. What matters more than how much money you earn is how you use it. At times, those who spend all that they earn will struggle to put aside what they make for their future. However, one who saves and invests well shall build wealth over time regardless of the mode of their earnings. What he establishes is that a good financial attitude leads to more financial success. It is practically true for many people's lives that poverty is because of earning less but no financial discipline. Take, for example, the case: "I do not earn enough money," when no record of where they put their money is observed. It reveals a lack of good financial culture rather than low income. An organized person who accounts for every expenditure and saves at least a fraction of his earnings will be better off regardless of the income level.

It must be understood that any person's financial status is directly proportional to the mental thought process of the person. There are individuals who generally view money as something positive and actively pursue increasing their assets step by step. On the other hand, there are individuals who passively blame a cause like bad luck or inflation for their poor financial condition. This mentality needs to change, and taking charge of money has to be managed with planning and discipline as the key to financial success.

Jese ki main kehti hu, dhan ko sahi tareeke se sambhalne ki soch hi aapki aarthik sthiti mein sudhar laa sakti hai.

Your financial philosophy, on the other hand, is your guiding principle in terms of how to use money. It's your personal beliefs about money and how it should feature in your life. There are people who see money as just a means to an end; others see it as a tool to gain financial freedom and security. In actual fact, your financial philosophy shapes the way you earn, save, and invest.

I personally feel, that there are three major financial philosophies which people are naturally wired to follow:

- Earn as much as you can and manage the earnings well: This is where this particular set of people zeroes in on getting the most money they can have at their disposal and then frugally using that money. They regulate their expenses, save regularly, and invest in assets that appreciate in value over time. This is one of the best ways to achieve long-term financial security and prosperity.

- Earning sufficiently and just in time: Those persons are always good at earning just as much that would cover their expenses. They would not aim to build a lot of wealth but can put down enough to give a supporting life and show financial ability in the way of a secure and stable life.

- Earn-money attitude: They don't attach much importance to earning or managing money. They think that it is not of much importance, or they don't need to care about it. Such a mindset will make them fail when it comes to managing money because they never save or invest in the right places.

Your financial philosophy may work for or against you to realize your goals. Knowing which philosophy you follow and, if not conducive, adjusting it will enhance your financial planning perspective. I feel that if one adopts an active financial philosophy where saving and investing is a way of life, then they become more financially free.

Role of Savings and Investment

The most basic element of being successful in finance is how to balance the flow of income with savings and investments. One of the major underlying points relates to the fact that even with a modest income, regular saving of a fraction of that should be your objective. It isn't about how much you earn; it is about how much you can save and invest for the future.

One thing which all success do have in common is that they always save and invest a part of their income. Whether he earns ten rupees or one lakh rupees, the individual has it as a habit to keep his money aloof for savings and investments. That is how they eventually build their wealth. The word is a disciplined approach to money whereby spending only what is necessary, so the rest is invested in assets that will grow in worth.

The significant point here is that any sort of investment should be understood first. Saving in a bank account is, of course, important for short-term purposes and does not create a very significant return in the long run. There are other investment options that one should look at for wealth growth:

- Stocks and Mutual Funds - These usually have higher returns but are risky together. However, if invested prudently and over a long time, equities and mutual funds can significantly build up your wealth.

- Insurance Plans. Any financial plan mustn't forget to include any coverage from life insurance or health insurance to secure the participant with some form of emergency protection.

- Property or Real Estate: Another protected investment to generate wealth in the long term is through property since property appreciates with time.

Savings and investments strike a balance wherein your money works for you. Typically, plan for short-term and long-term goals, like saving for an emergency fund, educating your child, or planning for retirement.

Emergency and Inflation Preparation

Any financial planning should, therefore, consider what happens in case of inflation and unexpected expenses. Inflation is the increase in the cost of goods and services, and because of it, money devalues gradually over time. This means that the same money amount would buy less the next year. Income and savings must, therefore, rise every year to keep pace with inflation.

You should regularly review your financial plans taking into consideration inflation. From this, the need will be to ensure that your savings and investments return a value that is higher than the inflation level. In essence, as such a saving, investment in stocks or mutual funds provides returns that usually exceed the inflation rate. This is because your money continues to grow rather than decrease in value.

Besides inflation, unexpected expenses such as an emergency medical bill or loss of employment can quite significantly impact your finances. That's the reason why maintaining an emergency fund is quite important. An emergency fund is a pool of savings you can draw upon when faced with unexpected happenings. Financial gurus advise that an emergency fund should be enough for at least 6 months of living expenses. This helps you ride financial shocks without going into debt or otherwise giving up on your long-term investments.

Mindset and Success

Success in financial planning will be dependent on the mindset with which one approaches matters coupled with discipline in handling money matters. Income is of course crucial, but the winning edge is in being able to save, invest, or plan for the future.

Successful people keep their eyes on the big picture. They realize that each rupee saved and invested is added to their goals. They do not shy away from saving for future expenses money one needs to save for a house, children's education, or retirement. They are prepared for uncertainty-like the rise in inflation and emergencies-such that their financial future remains sound.

Safalta ke liye, yojna banana zaroori hai.

Life Stages of Financial Planning

Financial planning is a dynamic process that evolves at different stages of life. Starting from early adulthood to old age, the human passes through several phases when there is a change in his or her financial needs, responsibilities, and priorities. It is crucial to manage money at every stage in life for successful and secure finances. The following section emphasizes the major four life stages and how financial planning can be customized according to the specific needs at every stage.

Early Adulthood (20-30 Years): Foundation Building

In early adulthood, any human being is only getting started to join a career or venture into their own business. At this stage, one would generally have fewer financial burdens and a greater ability to save and invest. Consequently, building a sound financial foundation should be the focus of this phase.

- Career Development and Income Growth: The twenties often characterize a stage of skill accumulation, work experience building, and developing a career track. There is usually job hopping during this stage as one seeks to change for greater prospects in life. This is beneficial in terms of income increases but should be weighed against greater living costs in bigger cities.

- Saving and Investment: This is the ideal time to develop the saving and investing habit. Even though income can be low, the need is to start early. Savings invested in equities, mutual funds, or retirement accounts bring great reaping benefits due to compounding; the earlier one starts, the more time their investments have to grow.

Indeed, most of them start taking student loans or debts in whatever form. If they can attain it, then debt repayment should come first before saving for the future; otherwise, financial stress will greet them in later life.

Just by working on one's career to ensure proper savings and savvy investment, the 20s are set for an even greater stable future.

Mid-Career (30-45 Years): Income Generation and Managing Responsibilities

The mid-career period, between 30 and 45 years, is typically at the peak earning years. People during this stage are well-established in their careers and are expected to earn very high incomes. Then again, it also involves a lot of financial responsibilities, particularly from family commitments, mortgages, and childcare.

- Balancing one's income with expenses: It becomes challenging in this phase to keep income manageable with larger expenses. According to me, controlling necessary expenses and discretionary expenses is very important as both of them have a bearing on financial health. A person should not overspend; if income has increased, then the budget also needs to be more than the spending limit. Proper tracking of expenses and following a budget help avoid overspending.

- Saving for the Long Term: It is the period when a person is supposed to save for long-term goals like children's education, buying a house, and retirement. This security can be achieved through long-term growth assets like mutual funds, stocks, or real estate. Such an individual is also likely to have ensured life insurance and adequate health insurance coverage as well as protection against large undesired events.

- Savings and Debt Reduction At midcareer: Save at least 70 percent of your income. At this stage, you should be debt-free or almost debt-free. Pay off high-interest debts, such as credit cards or personal loans, as soon as possible. Paying off debt relieves money to save and invest in the future and lessens stress because it places individuals closer to retirement.

This stage is characterized by the management of growing financial demands against saving or investing for later life security. By managing their expenses and making smart investments, people can continue to grow their wealth and get ready for the next phase in their life.

Pre-Retirement (45-60 Years): Financial Independence

At the pre-retirement stage or age, 45 to 60 years, they now begin to shift their financial concentration to financial independence. At this juncture, many would have seriously thought about retirement and had saved considerable amounts in the bank to sustain them since they were no longer working.

- Maximizing Savings and Investments: Maximize contributions to retirement accounts and other investment vehicles. Assess your financial situation, how you are doing in reaching the level of old age desired, and whether to increase savings and curtail unwanted expenses.

- Retirement Planning: The pre-retirement period is a very important planning period for retirement fund provision. People need to calculate how much their recurrent monthly expenses would be in order to be able to maintain their desired post-retirement lifestyle with the confidence that they have sufficient savings or pension funds. It may also prove to be the time for living expense reduction, for example, paying off remaining mortgages or other loans and concentrating on putting together a good-sized retirement fund.

- Health and Medical Planning: With growing older, health issues become an ever-increasing concern. I feel we need to address how health insurance is necessary to save a considerable sum for medical expenses in case they are required to seek treatment. A portion of their retirement savings should be saved uniquely for health care costs so they do not become a burden when they retire.

There is a higher focus on achieving retirement security through increasing savings, eliminating debt, and preserving pre-retirement money.

Retirement and Beyond (60+ Years): Preserving and Saving Wealth

This is the stage of retirement, which involves a concern to preserve and ensure that the savings can be sustained until one's retirement. I agree that financial planning does not stop when one retires but instead gets onto careful budgeting, letting the cost of living expenses wind down, and healthcare.

In fact, in retirement, the concern is living off savings, pensions, or investments. A good realistic budget that provides for living expenses, health care, and all else is necessary. retirees are wise to exercise careful management of their withdrawals from retirement accounts to avoid spending too much money too soon and outliving their income.

- Conservation of Wealth: At this point, wealth preservation should be pursued. In this stage, the retiree can take on more conservative investments since there are fewer years for redemption when the markets should have crashed harder. Proper wealth management during retirement enhances the guarantee of financial security in old age.

- Health and Emergency Savings: As discussed above, health care becomes one of the largest expenses in retirement. Savings for health insurance or any other arrangements for emergencies could prevent retirement savings from being depleted.

Now, this is where a great deal of the money worked up over the previous decades needs to be put to work without wasting it.

Financial planning is a lifelong process, and every phase of life has a different approach to handling finances. From the establishment laid during young adulthood to financial independence before retirement, each phase poses its share of special difficulties and opportunities. Knowing how to plan effectively throughout all these stages can amount to a well-secured life of good financial stability, leading to an unshaken prosperous life. The essence of success in life is not earning money but managing it well during one's lifetime.

Exercise:

Q1: Financial Mindset Reflection

Instructions: Reflect on your current mindset about money. Consider the following questions:

- What financial philosophy do you follow? (e.g., Earn as much as you can and manage the earnings well, Earning sufficiently and just in time, Earn-money attitude)
- How do you typically make decisions about money? (e.g., Do you spend impulsively, save regularly, invest for the future?)
- What financial habits could you improve to move towards greater financial success? (e.g., Start saving a percentage of income, reduce discretionary spending, invest in assets that appreciate)
- What would it take for you to adopt a more proactive approach to saving and investing? (e.g., Create a budget, set specific financial goals, educate yourself about investment options)

Q2: The Financial Plan

Create a simple financial plan for yourself using the following steps:

1. Current Income and Expenses:
    - List your monthly income.
    - List your regular monthly expenses (e.g., rent, utilities, groceries).

2. Savings Goals:
    - Set a goal for how much you want to save each month.
    - Decide how much of your savings will go into long-term investments (e.g., stocks, mutual funds) and how much will go into a short-term savings fund (e.g., emergency fund).
3. Investment Strategy:
    - Research and choose one type of investment you're interested in (e.g., real estate, stocks, mutual funds).
    - Set a long-term goal (e.g., retirement, child's education) and determine how much you need to invest each month to reach that goal.
4. Emergency Fund:
    - Determine how much you want to set aside for unexpected expenses.
    - Set a target amount (e.g., 6 months of living expenses) and create a plan to build it over the next year.
5. Review and Adjust:
    - Set a reminder to review your financial plan every 6 months.
    - Adjust your savings rate or investment strategy as needed.

<table>
<tr><th colspan="2">Category</th><th>Amount</th><th>Notes</th></tr>
<tr><td rowspan="2">Income & Expenses</td><td>Current monthly Income</td><td></td><td></td></tr>
<tr><td>Regular monthly expenses</td><td></td><td></td></tr>
<tr><td rowspan="2">Savings goal</td><td>Short term savings</td><td></td><td></td></tr>
<tr><td>Long term savings</td><td></td><td></td></tr>
<tr><td>Investment strategy</td><td>Real estate/stocks/mutual funds/retirement plans</td><td></td><td></td></tr>
<tr><td>Emergency funds</td><td>Living expenses of atleast 6 months</td><td></td><td></td></tr>
</table>

Chapter 3: The Fundamentals of Money Management

Money management is the core of financial security and success in life. Proper money management hinges on the comprehension of basic elements of personal and national economics: assets, liabilities, inflation, taxation, and debt management. In this chapter, we will discuss these basic financial elements and suggest ways for you to achieve financial balance and security. *Aapke paise sahi tarah se sambhalna aapki zimmedaari hai. Par ghabraiye mat, mera haath pakad kar bas chal lijiye, manzil zyada dur nahi hai.*

Know Inflation

Inflation is the most significant single factor affecting the life of a human being vis-à-vis his financial life. Essentially, it describes the state of the general price level of goods and services in an economy over a period of time and reduces the purchasing power of money. Today, something that costs ₹100 may cost ₹150 in a few years. Though one may not be able to control inflation, its effects can certainly be managed through proper financial planning.

Different people are affected differently by inflation due to the kind of financial position one is in. The cost of living increases, particularly on basic needs, such as food, transportation, and housing. People must then work out their budget to maintain the same purchasing power against the effects of inflation. This can be achieved by saving more money and investing it in enterprises that give returns much higher than the inflation rate. It will not suffice to merely keep the money in any low-interest savings account because, with time, inflation will be eating into its value. Rather, investing through stocks, mutual funds or real estate can help to produce returns that beat inflation.

The other important budgeting with inflation rate is also done. In the book, if your current inflation rate is around 7%, then you must budget for the increase your budget needs to account for that high rate. For example, if your monthly expenses are ₹100, plan for at least ₹107 or more to prepare for the effect of inflation.

Leaving unattended the raging inflation and not making proper adjustments in the finances can lead to the greatest difficulties, seriously affecting the state of the budget in the future. So, there is an urgent need to construct an active attitude regarding inflation control on the basis of knowledge of what inflation does in everyday life, as well as financial planning.

Banks and Interest Rates

The banking system plays a very important role in the financial life of an individual and firms. Banks offer savings as well as deposit options but also loans for purchasing homes, education, and expansion of business among many other reasons. The interest rate charged on loans is very critical because it determines the amount you will pay over time.

The RBI controls interest rates for all Indian banks. Interest rates do fluctuate with the economic circumstances. Even though an increase in interest rate by the RBI results in increased cost and repayment of loans, it is still essential to inform borrowers - a partly loan-dependent individual - about how interest rates affect their balance sheet.

Most people take loans, but that should not be done indiscriminately. The quantum of expenses towards loan repayment need not be more than 25-30% of the amount of your monthly income. Therefore, if your salary for the month is ₹20,000, loan repayment should not exceed ₹6,000, because improper management of loans leads to debt accumulation, which will have a negative impact on your financial health.

Besides loan management, one should also be aware of the savings and fixed deposit interest offered by banks. These usually are much below inflation, and therefore bank saving alone may not be the efficient way to grow wealth. Diversify investments in mutual funds or stocks that provide better returns to grow wealth far faster.

Managing Assets and Liabilities

Assets were one of the concepts that really confused me when learning about personal finance. But when I unpacked it, it all started making good sense. Here's how it boils down: Something that belongs to me that either puts money in my pocket or is worth more tomorrow than it was today is an asset. For example, the house I own, my savings, stocks, or even the business I have invested in-all these are assets as they either generate some income or appreciate in value.

Now, liabilities are like the monetary weights I carry. They're my debts or obligations sucking money out of my pocket. The home loan, car loan, and even credit card balance all represent my liabilities. These represent the money owed, along with monthly payments that steadily continue to siphon off my cash available.

This is like a balancing act between what I own and what I owe. Increasing assets while reducing liabilities will be a great thing for me. When I pay off my home loan, the house will become a full asset and will no longer be a liability holding me down. The more I grow and shrink my assets, the more I will be financially stable.

Let me tell you the story of two friends, Rohan and Sameer, who both vied for their place in the grand expanse of personal finance. Rohan was always an enthusiast with fast cars and gadgetry. He worked hard, then always spent it on things that he thought would make him happy, just about as soon as he saved a little. Then, there was a smartphone on credit or even a high-end holiday paid through a personal loan. Rohan would never give much of a thought to his future financial well-being; money to him, is there to be spent and he will work out the rest of it whenever there is a problem.

Sameer, however, thought differently. He also loved life, but for him, money was rather an arithmetic affair. Sameer's father had always told him to begin building assets: things that would assist him in growing his wealth over time. Though not like Rohan, Sameer had a quiet confidence about himself when it came to anything related to money.

One day, after Sameer saw Rohan worriedly juggling the check for another credit card bill, he asked Rohan to sit down. "Rohan, have you ever thought of why you are always stressed about money despite having a pretty great job?"

Rohan shrugged. "It's just the way life is, Sameer. I mean, what can you do? Bills pile up, right?"

Sameer leaned in, "This doesn't have to be so, my friend. You see, managing money is a matter of balance with one's assets and liabilities."
Rohan looked lost. "Assets? Liabilities? What do you mean?"

Sameer's smile. "Let me simplify it for you. An asset is something which puts money in your pocket or appreciates with time, be it a house, stocks, or even a business. Liabilities are those things which amount to debts or take out money from your pocket. Such could be loans and credit card debt, or even a car that loses its value."

Rohan nodded slowly. "Okay. But what do I do with this now?

Sameer continued, "Right now, you're spending on liabilities, things like your credit cards and personal loans. They may give you short-term satisfaction, but in the long run, they are draining your money out. When you do that, you will always feel as if you're behind. The key to financial stability is that you add more assets and cut out on liabilities."

"So, what should I do?" Rohan inquired, fascinated but unsure.

Let's start small, Sameer said. "First, think of your biggest liabilities. For instance, that new car you bought-it's not an asset because cars lose value over time. Plus, you took a loan to buy it, right? So, now you're paying interest on something that's not appreciating. If you had invested that money in stocks or mutual funds, you'd be growing your wealth.

Rohan furrowed his brow. "I never thought of it that way."

Sameer nodded. "I know. Think about a house. A house can be an asset because over time, its value usually appreciates. Plus, you could rent it out and earn money from it. The mortgage you took to buy it is a liability, yes, but if the house appreciates and generates income, it eventually becomes a net asset.".

"So, it's buying something whose worth will increase, right?" asked Rohan.

"Exactly," said Sameer. "The objective is to increase your assets and reduce your liabilities. The more assets you gain the more secure you are in terms of finances in the long term. It's all like planting trees that take years to see results, but once you do, it provides shade for life. Liabilities are as if weeds-they can cover your entire garden if you don't tend to them, always asking for attention and your resources will begin to drain."

Rohan finally started to understand "So, I need to stop buying things on credit and invest in things that make me money?"

Sameer smiled. "Yes, but it is not all about cutting off all spending. It is about being smart with your money. You don't have to live a boring life. You can still enjoy things, but you have to be more conscious of whether you are buying something that will drain your resources or build them."

Over time, Rohan changed his way of living. He stopped using his credit card for things he did not need. He was paying off debts little by little. Instead of buying another car on a loan, he invested in a small apartment and rented it out. It was not all overnight, but gradually, he felt safe. He no longer became stressed each time the bill came in, and for the first time ever, savings began to appear in his account.

One day, Rohan and Sameer met for coffee. "You know, you were right," Rohan admitted. "It's all about balance-additional assets and liability reduction. I feel like I am now in control of my finances, and this feels nice."

Sameer smiled. "Well, glad you are noticing the difference. The more assets you build, the more freedom you will gain. And believe me, the peace of mind from true financial security is worth much more than any gadget."
In the end, they both learned lessons about money, but it was Rohan who would become wiser and discover that by changing his approach he could enjoy life *and* secure his financial future: it was not a

question of living in denial or deprivation but building up a sound foundation of assets to sustain him for the rest of his life.

And that's the story of how balanced assets and liabilities turned Rohan's life around, one smart choice at a time.

Debt Management Strategies

Management of debt is an important part of managing your money. While debts are sometimes also borrowed through loans, too much debt could always mean financial stress and insecurity. Hence, it is very vital that you have a plan for managing debt.

It's recommended that loan payments should never exceed 25-30% of one's monthly income. Whenever it exceeds the limit, then financial stress develops and there is a problem with saving and investing. Then, at least one should pay back more with high-interest debt, such as credit cards or personal loans that one can accumulate really fast and become uncontrollable.

Debt consolidation is another form of effective management of various loans. When debts are combined into one loan at a lower rate of interest, the person can make fewer payments each month and also manage his or her finances much better.

It is also risky to go for unnecessary debt. Most people take loans and forget the long-term financial implications, leading to debt burdens that they cannot handle. This is critical to evaluate before taking a loan: does the loan really need to be taken or does it fit my financial plan?

Local Economic Conditions and Crisis Management

Lastly, personal finance is impacted by local economic conditions. Inflation rates, cost of living, and economic stability are quite high from city to state and state to city. For example, living expenses in tier 1 cities are several times higher than in smaller towns; thus, people living in large cities should plan for a higher amount of money.

A sudden crisis, such as the one brought about by the COVID-19 pandemic, can easily drain one's personal finances. Economic downturns, job losses, or medical expenses may put a person off track even if he or she has made the best of financial plans. Hence, an emergency fund covering at least 6 months of living expenses is critical in not falling prey to all such eventualities. Such a fund acts as a financial safety net during crisis times.

Knowing the economic surroundings in the region and preparing for emergencies will help individuals better overcome economic hard times.

Main bas itna kehna chahti hu ant mein...

Money management is essentially a comprehensive tool, and therefore it engages in understanding several aspects of finance such as inflation, taxation, assets, liabilities, and debt management. It is through proactive awareness of these factors that individuals can hope for security and stability in finances. Assets and liabilities must be effectively managed and only then with proper planning regarding inflation, taxes, and debt.

Exercise:

Q1: Multiple-Choice Questions (MCQs)

1. What is inflation primarily responsible for?
   - a) Increasing the value of money
   - b) Reducing the purchasing power of money
   - c) Increasing interest rates
   - d) Increasing wages for all employees

2. Which of the following is considered an asset?
   - a) Car loan
   - b) House you own
   - c) Credit card debt
   - d) Monthly rent payment

3. How does inflation affect your budgeting?
   - a) It makes your savings grow faster
   - b) It increases the cost of living, requiring adjustments in your budget
   - c) It reduces your debt payments
   - d) It has no effect on budgeting

4. What is the general rule for managing loan repayment?
   - a) Loan repayment should be no more than 50% of your monthly income.

- b) Loan repayment should be no more than 25-30% of your monthly income.
- c) There is no limit to loan repayment.
- d) Loan repayment is not necessary as long as you can pay it off eventually.

5. What is debt consolidation?
   - a) Taking a loan to pay off other loans at a higher interest rate
   - b) Combining multiple loans into one loan at a lower interest rate
   - c) Ignoring debt payments until they are forgiven
   - d) Borrowing money to invest in assets

Q2: Identifying Assets and Liabilities

In the list below, identify which items are assets and which are liabilities.

1. Home loan
2. Stocks you own
3. Car loan
4. Business you run
5. Credit card debt
6. Personal savings account
7. Rental property generating income
8. Furniture and appliances

Chapter 4: The Call for Financial Literacy

Financial literacy is the foundation on which to build wealth and long-term security, yet it is one of the least understood and most grossly neglected aspects of education in the world today. Without a sound understanding of basic money management concepts, even a high income can vanish overnight, leaving families staring into the abyss of a financial crisis. Honest to goodness, no amount of money makes a difference if not managed right. The heart of financial literacy is recognizing the ability to distinguish between liabilities and assets and growing the former while decreasing the latter. These seem to be simple principles but have a massive impact. This chapter will delve into the notion of financial literacy and why it is so imperative to learn such tenets for a prosperous future in finance. *Yeh chotti chotti cheeze karein se aapki zindagi mein bade bade badlav aa sakte hai. Agar bharosa nahi hai, toh khud azma ke dekh lijiye.*

Let us think that you won a sudden lottery of two lakh rupees. That's a sizeable amount, isn't it? You start imagining everything that you could buy with that money-a new car, a holiday abroad, fancy gadgets. But before you know it, when the money is gone, spent just as soon as it was earned, and a week has passed by, you are again at square one handling your monthly budget. That's the reality for many who cannot even imagine how their money can be managed in a bigger way. This is the ultimate case of financial illiteracy.

Money management is not about having more money; it is about knowing what to do with what you have. *Paisa sahi se istemal karna, bachana, aur sahi tarah se bachana, yahi saara khel hai.* Financial education is curiously absent from the curriculum in our society. Whether it's at primary school or a university, a student is hardly ever taught how to manage his or her personal finances. Except for commerce and finance streams, subjects such as science, arts, and engineering bypass this crucial life skill. It doesn't come as a surprise, then, that most educated people are financial illiterates. Consequence? Poor money management skills and their disastrous long-term after-effects are more common than we think.

According to the report by the Reserve Bank of India, only 27 per cent of men and 24 per cent of women in India are financially literate. This statistic is really alarming for India, which is growing its economy rapidly. It is more than just a personal goal, but a societal need: financial literacy. When people manage their money well, they also contribute to the stability of an economy as well as to improving their living standards. But how does one start with financial education?

At its heart, financial literacy is about three very simple notions: income, spending, and saving. But to truly manage your money, you need to know two other concepts that are critical to that purpose: assets and liabilities. These two terms are deceptively simple, but they hold the key to truly long-term financial success.

An asset, for example, is something that puts money in your pocket either directly by generating income or indirectly by appreciating in value over time. Think about real estate that appreciates, stocks that pay dividends, or a business that turns a profit. A liability, on the other hand, is something that takes money out of your pocket-debt, loans, or financial obligations that have got to be paid. Getting to know the difference between the two is really important, as it influences your financial strategy.

For example, you could imagine that you are a salaried employee who earns a fixed amount every month. Your paycheck is not an asset, it is your income. Now, suppose you decide to spend that money on buying a car or even a house. What you have done here is acquire an asset. If, however, you borrow the money from somebody else to make this purchase, then what you have also done is incur a liability: you now have a loan. The car or the house may appreciate in value, so it is now an asset, but draining your finances dry until it is paid.

A businessman is in the same boat. When he purchases equipment, office space, or raw materials, they become an asset to him as they will increase the revenues of the business and make it more profitable. The loans he seeks to finance are liabilities. In both cases- whether it is an individual or a businessman-the bottom line is the same: one must accumulate more assets and reduce liabilities.

It is a simple principle: the more assets you have relative to liabilities, the wealthier and more financially secure you are. Then there are people who seem to just keep on accumulating liabilities without understanding how to offset liabilities with assets. Credit cards are one of the most common forms of liability. They may seem rather convenient in the short term, but if not managed carefully, they quickly get out of hand, leading to overwhelming debt.

So how does one achieve financial stability and freedom? The answer lies in balancing your assets and liabilities. The ideal financial management strategy follows what we call the "one-to-one rule." That is, for every ₹1 of liability you take on, you should have at least ₹1 of assets to offset it. If your liabilities exceed your assets, you're headed for financial trouble. On the other hand, if the assets are more than the liabilities, then you stand good as a healthy financial state.

Let's break it down to a simple formula as well:

Assets / Liabilities = 1 (Ideal Management)

- Assets / Liabilities < 1 (Poor Management)
- Assets / Liabilities > 1 (Excellent Management)

The objective must always be to increase your assets while keeping your liabilities in check. This actually means the repayment of loans much faster than required, thinking less about unnecessary debt, and investing where value will rise. Supposing you took a 15-year loan in purchasing a home; you try to repay the loan within 10 or 12 years. This will reduce the amount of interest you will pay over time but also increase your financial security much faster.

Ab yahi baat aap ek vyapar mein bhi lagake samaj sakte hai. A wise businessman understands how to level off his assets and liabilities. Business assets will include cash in reserve, owned property, and machinery. Assets also include loans and outstanding debts. A business owner wise about finances will always try to reduce liabilities by cutting down expenses and debt clearance as soon as possible.

A proper savings plan for both people and entrepreneurs creates wealth. Saving does not mean putting away part of your income. Rather, it's the appropriate investment of that saving so that you could earn a return from it. This wisdom thus says, "Savings lead to investments, and investments lead to wealth." But the catch is, that saving money in a bank account is not that easy. The actual wealth-building process comes through a return on investment. For example, if you're getting 3-4% interest from a fixed deposit, however, you're compensating 7% on a loan, your net return turns negative. Such financial misuse can lead to a gradual erosion of your wealth.

For a person not to fall into these pitfalls, one must be financially literate. That does not make one an economics or finance expert; however, it calls for some basic appreciation of how money management works. These constitute the understanding of what assets and liabilities are and how debt can be reduced as well as learning about making good investments.

The journey to financial freedom is definitely not a sprint- it's a marathon with much discipline and patience and a solid understanding of how money works. Taking the assets in today's lifetime and adding eroding liabilities combined with some smart decisions made upon investments might lead to stable and secure finances for anybody. And although financial literacy might not be one of the subjects taught in school, it is never too late to learn. Financial education opens a lifetime of wealth and independence.

You should be able to differentiate between liabilities and assets to properly care for your personal finances. The concept of liability reduction while enhancing the levels of assets, in essence, stands for solid financial management and wealth building. Many people increase their wealth while most are busy trying to reduce their liabilities. We discuss in this section how to reduce liabilities and increase assets. We offer insight and methodology that will guide an individual toward long-term financial stability and growth.

Understanding Liabilites

To know how to reduce liabilities, first understand what a liability is. Liability is a kind of financial obligation or debt that you or any business owes to any other party. In short, these could be credit card debts, loans-mortgage or automobile loans, student debts, or any form of personal loan. For all intents and purposes, liabilities are the cash that is draining out of your pocket, thus exhausting your pocket.

Liabilities are generally classified into two types: good liabilities and bad liabilities.

- **Good liabilities** include debts, such as mortgages or student loans, that may be referred to as investments in future earning capacity or asset buildup. An example of this is a person buying a house on a mortgage: it can be termed as an investment because houses generally appreciate in value over time.
- **Bad liabilities** involve consumer debt such as credit card balances or personal loans that are used for things other than investments and, therefore, have a relatively high-interest cost with no long-term financial payback.

Reduction of bad liabilities is paramount to improving the health of one's financial life and freeing up resources for asset accumulation.

Tools for Liability Reduction

<u>Budgeting and Expense Monitoring</u>

Budgeting and tracking your expenses are two important steps to avoid losing control of your finances. A budget, for example, can be thought of as the roadmap for your money; it tells you how to put money in each of the categories that come across-such as rent, groceries, savings, and entertainment. That way, you will not overspend and have savings for future goals.

Expense tracking may be defined as a process whereby one tracks every single transaction to see where money goes. Without a careful review of spending habits, you end up wasting money on small expenses that you never even think about. Regular review of your spending habits can reveal areas where you might be wasting money, which leads to changes. You will not randomly guess where the money has disappeared, but instead, actively manage your money to save more, lower debt, and grow health. Budgeting and expense monitoring are indeed great tools to be together for building financial discipline and achieving long-term goals.

For example, if you use your credit card to pay off a balance, you may have expenditures, such as $100 per month on coffee or memberships that you pay for streaming.

Debt Consolidation

Consolidation of debt is a process where a number of debts are consolidated into a single loan usually at a lower rate of interest. This makes your debt repayment much easier and often decreases the total interest you have to pay on the consolidated amount. For example, if you owe money on multiple credit cards with high interest rates, consolidation into a personal loan at a lower rate of interest would make it easier to repay.

Consolidation streams expenses into one payment instead of several individual payments. It also prevents late payments and further expands liabilities with the compounding of penalties and fees.

The Snowball and Avalanche Methods

When working on liabilities, two very common methods are the debt snowball and debt avalanche methods.

- The debt snowball method is paying off the smallest debt first, but paying the minimum payments on others. When one of the small debts is paid, the money that previously went to the small debt is then moved over to the next smallest debt and so on. It can be a good psychological motivator because you see those debt balances knocked out, even though it doesn't always save you the most money in interest.

- This is a debt avalanche- you pay off your debt with the highest interest first, so you're paying the minimum on other debts. Then, when that high-interest debt gets paid off, you go to the next one. This is going to save you money over time because you will pay less in interest; however, it seems like longer before the first debt goes away.

References – Dave Ramsey – The snowball and avalanche method

Although both options reduce liabilities, both have different intentions and are useful in their own ways. Depending upon whether one needs to maximize psychological satisfaction or financial optimality, the choice between these two options can be made as follows.

Refinance Debt

One of the great financial choices I have made to date is to refinance my debt. There were a couple of loans carrying high-interest rates-credit cards and a personal loan-and they really weighed on me every month. It was a feeling of paying payments that were getting nowhere. Therefore, I started researching refinancing options.
Refinancing simply means taking out a new loan at a lower interest rate to pay off debts with higher rates on them, so when I was doing this, I had the chance to consolidate my loans into one payment that would be easier to manage, and the decrease in interest would really enable me to save a huge amount over time.

It wasn't a complicated process either. I compared different lenders, found one with much better terms, and applied. Once approved, I used the new loan to clear the old ones. That immediately reduces my monthly payments, gives me more breathing room within my budget, and puts me on a faster path to becoming debt-free. It was absolutely great to see real progress in the finances.

Steering Clear of New Liabilities

One of the easiest ways to reduce liabilities is simply to cease adding new liabilities. For some, this may mean cutting down on the use of credit cards, or finding the discipline to avoid borrowing from a personal bank for frivolous purchases, but above all, avoiding payday loans that always carry astronomically high interest rates.

If you find it extremely difficult to quit using credit cards, you may consider a change to a debit card or imposing a stricter limit on the credit card. This way, you will avoid hitting a big pile of high-interest debt, which tends to spiral out of control too quickly. In another vein, you would establish an emergency fund to avoid dipping into credits should the unexpected happen.

Gathering Assets

Now that we've touched on ways to reduce liabilities, it's time to discuss the other side of the financial success coin and the ways you can add assets. Assets are things that place money in your pocket. But Begin with Savings.

Building assets begins with having a saving habit. You cannot invest or buy assets if you have nothing in the capital account. Simple as this sounds, "pay yourself first" is one of the best ways to build wealth: take some money from your paycheck for savings and investment before you spend any money on anything else. Leading financial gurus recommend saving at least 10% to 20% of your income.

Some of the good uses of an automated savings plan include finding money to save and investing in a savings or investment account through transfers arranged from your checking account. Such funds may not be easily spent as people try to avoid touching the money.

Investment in Stock Markets

Probably one of the easiest ways to expand your wealth is through a stock market investment. Shares comprise stocks as a part or percentage of ownership in an entity, and long-term investments have tendently been greater over time than any bonds or savings accounts.

You don't have to be a financial advisor to invest. Many people begin with mutual funds or exchange-traded funds (ETFs), which offer a diversity of stocks. Taking off from small amounts of money that are contributed regularly into the stock market leads to the growth of sizable assets over time because of the compounding power.

Real Estate Investment

Real estate is another slightly more mainstream asset class approach. With real estate, unlike stocks, there's a possibility for income, since you can have rental income and appreciation in value as properties become more expensive. Moreover, you'll find tax savings when using a property, because interest paid on mortgages and property taxes are usually deductible.

Real estate investing doesn't need to require a huge amount of capital at the beginning. Many people start here with rental properties, and some even engage in "house hacking," where you live on one side of the property and rent out the other to pay the mortgage.

Creating a Business

Another asset-building activity is starting or investing in a business. And with all the money coming through, it has the potential to create cash flow and appreciate in value. A business, after all, can be ownership of one's financial destiny, whether a side hustle or a full-time endeavour.

All of these efforts, time and resources invested will surely make a business an asset that will produce much more in the long term than the effort it initially takes. Entrepreneurial success entrepreneurs use a business profit to invest in other assets, such as real estate or stocks.

Investment in Education and Skills

Although not very valuable, doubling your potential earnings increases the value of education and skills which can then be applied to other assets. The continuous update of knowledge and skills-particularly in more in-demand fields one's value in the job market enhances the probability of a business succeeding.

Not that one needs to interpret investing in education as going to college to achieve some level of formal degree because, with the proliferation of online courses, certifications, and other forms of specialized training that one can have, one is likely to generate better job opportunities and income, which will result in the accumulation of assets.

Diversification of Investments

It is from this point in your life that diversification becomes essential in keeping your wealth safe and steadily increasing. As the saying goes, "Don't put all your eggs in one basket." You will spread your investments to various asset classes- stocks, bonds, real estate, and perhaps commodities as well as minimize the risk that an individual asset class will become worthless and derail your finances.
Diversification also applies within asset classes. For example, if you are investing in stocks, you must hold shares across various industries, such as technology, health care, energy, etc. to neutralize the risks associated with sector-specific downturns.

.

Controlling Liabilities and Expanding Assets: Synergy

Paying off liabilities while increasing the assets is a good combination because, by paying for liabilities, the saved money can be re-dedicated to savings or investments. This boost in turn will accelerate your accumulation of assets, which now can generate returns and further help in paying for the liabilities, thus creating a positive feedback loop of financial growth.

For example, clearing out high-interest credit cards frees up a few hundred dollars a month. Instead of spending that money, you could invest it in the stocks or real estate sectors to increase your assets while preventing debt from piling up again.

Balancing liabilities and assets is what makes the journey towards wealth building and financial independence. *Inke beech mein santulan rakhna bahut zaroori hai.* The reduction of liabilities provides the much-needed breathing room, while increased assets form the base of long-term security. If people adopt some disciplined strategies such as budgeting, debt consolidation, and systematic investment, they not only get out of debt but also create a future of monetary affluence. The required mentality for this is that of long-term planning, continued improvement, and disciplined management of finances.

Exercise:

Q1. Financial Literacy Self-Assessment

Exercise:

Take a moment to assess your current understanding of financial concepts by rating yourself on a scale from 1 (not knowledgeable) to 5 (very knowledgeable) for each of the following areas:

- Understanding of assets and liabilities
- Ability to manage debt and loans
- Knowledge of saving and investing
- Budgeting skills
- Knowledge of financial products (e.g., insurance, mutual funds, credit cards)

Follow-up question:

- Based on your self-assessment, which areas would you like to improve? Set a goal for learning more about these areas and plan how you will do it.

Q2.Through the learnings of the chapter, you now know how to identify your assets and liabilities. List all of them in the table given below and calculate your net worth by using the given formula.

Assets	Liabilities
Total:	Total:
Total Assets - Total Liabilities = Net Worth	
Networth:	

Chapter 5: Discipline as the Road to Prosperity

Repeatedly in the corridors of success, you will hear the word "discipline". Whether the accomplishment is personal, financial, or long-term prosperity, discipline is at the heart of it all. What does discipline mean and how does it shape a path to prosperity? This chapter will delve into the nature of discipline, its two forms: external and self-discipline, and how successful people have applied it to their lives for outstanding results. We will also discuss the role of patience and perseverance in building long-term prosperity. With case studies of real lives, we will see how discipline can lead to significant personal and financial transformations.

Discipline vs Self-Discipline

In a nutshell, discipline just simply means following rules or standards. However, there are two main forms of disciplines: external and self. These two kinds of disciplines are different from each other, mainly because they function quite differently and play different roles in shaping one's journey to prosperity.

External discipline is when someone else controls your actions, such as through some kind of rules imposed on you by authority, deadlines set up for you by a superior, or by the expectations of your society. For instance, a company could have guidelines to report in and out during specific times. A teacher could demand that homework be done before a specific date. These are examples of external discipline—when someone else controls your actions through established boundaries.

While external discipline is not required for a stable, ordered environment, it is more likely to be a short-term tool for enforcing the status quo and dependent upon an external agent to be realized. The minute those external controls are removed, a person may return to his original behaviour. There is a certain degree of motivation for external discipline, but it can never be sustained over the long run.

Internal factors have become self-discipline. That is the personal commitment to one's own development and goals. Self-discipline, unlike external discipline, is cultivated within. It is that internal voice reminding you to keep going even when no one is watching. It means making choices that might be uncomfortable or difficult in the short term but accommodate your long-term needs.

Self-discipline is one of those most basic traits that distinguishes one who goes on to truly achieve success from those who seem to last only for a little while. The perfect example of self-discipline is a student studying for an exam not because the date is near, but because they want to do well. Similarly, saving a part of their salary every month by investing in the future though nobody forces them depicts self-control in handling finances. '*Aatma anushasan ki kunji hai*' is a proverb true across cultures.

This is where the difference between discipline and self-discipline stands out, for people act in other ways depending on various circumstances. Discipline majors rely more upon external circumstances to work. Self-discipline, however, thrives in any setting since it springs from personal values, vision, and determination.

Patience and Perseverance: The Road of Success

Discipline is pretty much associated with patience and persistence qualities that help achieve long-term goals success and prosperity. Instant gratification is one of those things that nowadays get so much praise in today's quick-timing world. However, the truth is that financial or personal prosperity rarely comes overnight. It is one of those things that take lots of time to build over time through constant actions, patience, and the will to persevere.

Patience is the resignation of the fact that you will not be able to achieve everything at once, and you will have to wait for the fruit of your toil. Fruits of patience are always sweet, says the proverb, and it is very aptly so there. In pursuing prosperity-investment, advancement in a profession, or any other form of bettering yourself, a patient man or woman is always in demand. For example, constructing an excellent investment portfolio typically involves years of prudent saving, savvy decision-making, and holding back from quick-fire maneuvers when market transactions hit critical lows. The urge to cash in quick returns has to be subdued so that wealth will grow with time.

Perseverance is the strength to press through obstacles and setbacks. Many people give up on their goals because the way ahead is riddled with failures. However, few great ones accept that there will be failures. They stick to it because they know failure is not a stop but a step to something much bigger. As Thomas Edison once famously said, "I have not failed. I've just found 10,000 ways that won't work." And then there is this level of perseverance that is rooted in this deep sense of discipline.

Let's look at the financial world for one concrete example. Warren Buffett is one of the richest men in the world, but he did not become rich overnight. His investment strategy, value investing, requires incredible patience and perseverance. The reason the wealth of Warren Buffett increased at a slow but steady pace was because he purchased stocks in companies he considered undervalued and held onto them for years-decades even. He let his disciplined approach to investing compound over time. And there's a reason why he is considered one of the greatest investors of all time it was his financial discipline alongside a patient and persevering mindset.

Of course, patience and perseverance are critical ingredients that go along with discipline in finance, career, and personal life. If these attributes are lacking, people tend to make impulsive decisions, which may hurt their long-term objectives. Prosperity comes when patience and discipline are exercised side by side.

Examples from Leading Individuals Who Follow Discipline in Life

There are enough examples to go around of very successful people who attribute their success to a disciplined lifestyle. Discipline is that invisible engine working behind the backdrop of success, which inspires every step and decision.

A recent example of such discipline was Indian cricketer Virat Kohli, hailed for incredible fitness and consistency on the field. *Inko toh bhala kon nahi jaanta?* That journey from nowhere has been, in itself, a story of extreme self-discipline. A transformation from a young, talented cricketer into a global superstar required extreme dedication to one's own fitness, diet, and training. Kohli's discipline isn't merely limited to the cricketing arena; it finds its reflection in routine practices of health and fitness, highly meticulous practice schedules, and disciplined ways of a leader have made him stand ahead. Kohli once said, "Self-belief and hard work will always earn you success." So very clear is that his success isn't just driven by talent but by the disciplined lifestyle he leads from day to day.

Then there's Elon Musk - the man who came up with the vision of Tesla, SpaceX, and Neuralink. Being very legendary to his countrymen, one wishes for nothing but the work ethic exemplified by Musk. He often refers to tedious hours in excess of 80 to 100 hours a week to keep dividing his time finely, precisely between each and every venture he sets his hand to. The disciplined schedule enables him to manage several billion-dollar companies simultaneously while pushing the boundaries of technology and innovation. Despite such numerous setbacks and failures, Musk remained disciplined and was keen on focusing on his long-term vision: What seemed impossible has finally been achieved, ranging from launching reusable rockets to making electric cars mainstream.

Let us take the life of Mahatma Gandhi who led India's freedom struggle through non-violence. Gandhi's discipline was not merely external but deeply internal. He followed an extremely rigid schedule: would wake up every morning, control his diet and lifestyle for a spartan right amount of flexibility, and staunchly adhere to the philosophy of non-violence despite huge provocation. With immense patience and perseverance, he achieved what many thought was impossible—that is, freedom for India from British rule. Strength does not come from physical capacity but from an indomitable will." This "indomitable will" was nothing but disciplined perseverance.

These examples depict that discipline does not mean just following the rules to play by rote but deliberate and thoughtful choices contributing to a greater goal. Whether it's Virat Kohli's fitness, Elon Musk's innovation, or Mahatma Gandhi's non-violent leadership, discipline is that constant force behind all their successes.

Long-term benefits of disciplined behaviour in personal and financial life

Although short-term discipline can be very restrictive and demanding, its long-term benefit is very great, especially in personal life and financial life. As for the personal life, it shows up through the place of good habits, such as regular exercise, mindful eating, and constant self-care. These habits over time make results such as healthier physical and mental fitness with an improved quality of life and longer life.

Take health for example. He may not appreciate what he is doing when subjected to a diet and regular exercise. For most times, all those changes are so minute that they cannot be appreciated within months or years. However, the increase of these disciplined choices will result in a stronger, healthier body and mind. Apart from health improvement, long run benefits of this sort of discipline mean more resilience on the part of a person's body.

Just like an individual, controlled behaviours in life, particularly financial life, induced by saving and budgeting to invest, reap marvellous long-term returns. Savings made monthly may appear trivial but, compounded over time, turn into gigantic amounts each year. The riches for financial freedom come from the consistency towards saving. *Chotte kadam se lamba raste tay ho sakta hai.* Small, consistent actions taken with discipline can lead to monumental changes over time.

For instance, take the investment in a diversified portfolio. The financial markets can change very drastically in the short term; a disciplined investor consistently puts money into his or her portfolio and does not emotionally overreact to market corrections. He or she will have high returns over the long term. It is just that the successful long-term investor keeps his discipline even when the market goes down, whereas panic sellers will always sell at a loss.

Discipline is the harbinger for continuous growth and self-improvement in personal development. While a novelist may write a little every day, she may not write a full novel in a month or a year. But that disciplined daily writing will eventually succeed in penning down her masterpiece. Such is the example of a musician who practices diligently even when he doesn't like it. He will slowly see improvement incrementally and master over time.

The long-term fruit of disciplined behaviour is not always visible to the naked eye but is impossible to avoid. Whether it happens through financial success or personal fulfillment or health, discipline is the opened door to enduring prosperity.

Discipline is not a habit or behaviour but a way of life. External discipline and self-discipline point out the difference between actual achievement being built from within. Accompanying patience and perseverance with this will help people overcome short-term hurdles to achieve long-term success. From the example of Virat Kohli, Elon Musk, and Mahatma Gandhi, we realize that unless we have determination, discipline alone may bring some extraordinary results. Discipline in personal development or health or finance paves the way for proper success at every stage. Prosperity is not a matter of fate; it's the outcome of stern effort and constant deliberate action.

Exercise:

Q1. Multiple Choice Questions (MCQs)

1. Which of the following best defines "self-discipline"?
   - a) Following rules set by others
   - b) Following internal commitments to personal goals
   - c) Doing tasks only when supervised
   - d) Adapting to society's rules without questioning them

2. What is the primary difference between external discipline and self-discipline?
   - a) External discipline is long-term, while self-discipline is short-term.
   - b) External discipline is imposed by others, while self-discipline is internal and self-motivated.
   - c) External discipline is not necessary for success, but self-discipline is.
   - d) Self-discipline is about following societal rules, whereas external discipline is personal.

3. Which of the following individuals is highlighted for their disciplined approach to work, particularly through long working hours?
   - a) Warren Buffett
   - b) Virat Kohli
   - c) Elon Musk

- d) Mahatma Gandhi

4. What does the proverb "Fruits of patience are always sweet" imply in the context of prosperity?
    - a) Instant gratification leads to long-term success.
    - b) Success comes quickly, but is not sustained.
    - c) Long-term success requires time, effort, and patience.
    - d) Financial success is always immediate when discipline is applied.

Q2. Case Study Review

Case Study:

Warren Buffett is known for his disciplined approach to investing, particularly his strategy of value investing, where he holds onto investments for long periods.

Exercise:

- What qualities of Warren Buffett's approach can be applied to your financial journey?
    - Focus on long-term goals.
    - Avoid impulsive reactions to market changes.
    - Build a diversified portfolio.

Follow-up:

- Explain how you could incorporate the principle of "discipline" into your own financial strategy.

Q3. Personalized Action Plan

Task:

Using the concept of discipline, create a 3-month action plan for achieving a personal goal (e.g., saving for a large purchase, losing weight, learning a new skill, etc.).

Instructions:

1. Define Your Goal: (Example: Save $1,000 for an emergency fund, learn a new language, etc.)
2. Identify the Steps: List specific, actionable steps to achieve your goal (e.g., save $100 each month, practice a language for 30 minutes a day).
3. Set Timelines: Create a realistic timeline for each step (e.g., save $100 by the end of month 1).
4. Track Progress: Define how you will track your progress (e.g., check savings balance weekly, review language practice progress).
5. Overcome Setbacks: Anticipate potential challenges and how you will stay disciplined through them.

Follow-up Question:

- How will you keep yourself motivated and disciplined throughout this process, and what are some strategies to avoid distractions or setbacks?

Chapter 6: The Habits of the Rich People

Can I ask you something? How many of you make it a habit to read the newspaper every day? Or picking up a book and spending some time getting lost in its pages? Chances are, only a handful will nod in agreement. But if I were to ask how many of you watch television or browse through social media every day, nearly everyone would raise their hands. This stark contrast reflects a bigger issue in our society and the choices we make in our daily habits. Former President of India, Dr. A.P.J. Abdul Kalam once said, "Every home in the country should have a small library with a minimum of ten books; this will create an urge among children to read." *Aur aakhir mein unhone kiya bhi vahi, jo unhone kaha.*

The man, even after accomplishing so many important tasks, lived a very simple life without even luxuries such as a TV, a car, or an air conditioner. Instead, the wealth was in the library filled with over 2,500 volumes. This is where the journey of success begins; value-added habits. One consistent activity, such as reading, can change not only the storehouse of knowledge of a person but the whole mindset. On the other hand, passive occupations such as spending hours in front of the television result in merely the wastage of precious time and do not contribute to personal growth in any meaningful manner. As goes the saying, 'Successful people have libraries; unsuccessful people have large-screen TVs.'

If heights of success in terms of wealth or personal fulfilment are your destinations, then discipline is your best friend. Warren Buffett, often named one of the world's richest men, epitomizes disciplined habits in his life. Here he is: Spending several hours every day reading newspapers, books and reports and inferring insights that have driven the overall financial decisions Buffett has made for decades.

Discipline is not only knowledge-building activities but practically all aspects of life, including financial habits. Buffett is famously quoted to have said, "Do not save what is left after spending; instead, spend what is left after saving." It brings in a reflection of the disciplined state of mind one must grow and preserve his wealth. *Chalo, ab ek nazar aapke din charya pe daalte hai.*

Reflect on your own day

Are you a well-planned person, or do you just go with the flow? A highly successful entrepreneurial venture like Infosys has been managed by its co-founder, Narayana Murthy. He believes in planning each day step-by-step. Murthy is known to chant his famous mantra of time management: "If I wake up early and set my targets, I will be in a better state of mind and get things done." His disciplined time allocation catapulted him to make Infosys a global giant. The hard truth: discipline isn't easy. It takes consistency, sacrifice, and belief in the rewards of longevity. Many people want a better life but do not offer themselves the commitment to change their habits. And the good news is that any individual can develop discipline with a mindset change. Start small. For example, start a diary habit. Writing down what you do each day may seem so mundane, but life-altering. Just imagine waking up every morning knowing just what you want to do and reviewing each night what you accomplished. It's much more about accountability and purpose than it is about checking a long list off.

Goals and Mentors Are Always Needed

What makes the world's most productive people successful? One important answer is: goal setting. Without goals, it's like drifting through a thick fog without a compass; there is no direction. Goals are like compasses and guide one toward an obvious destination.

For instance: Narayana Murthy founded Infosys along with a vision to establish a globally respected IT services company. Despite the numerous challenges thrown his way, this focused objective led him and his team to build one of the most successful enterprises in India.

However, objectives are not something that remains static; they change. They have to be worked out into smaller, actionable steps. This brings a sense of accomplishment and momentum. For example, if you want to save ₹10 lakhs in five years, start by saving ₹10,000 monthly. Small wins lead to bigger ones.

But even the most resolute, however, needs some push. Here comes into action a mentor. A mentor can give you some of the greatest insights you may ever have, encouragement, and constructive criticism. Most of the time, they have also been in your shoes as well or on that path already; hence, they can give you much-needed advice to speed you up further.

Warren Buffett gives full credit to his success by mentioning Benjamin Graham, the father of value investing, and states that much of his investment success is attributed to his mentor. "One way to describe it is to say that the mentor taught the protégé how to be disciplined, and disciplined means investment with a mind." Narayana Murthy credits his early mentors for teaching him the values of ethics, innovation, and perseverance.

But how do you find a mentor? First, you have to identify a person whose personal values and professional achievements inspire you. That could be your boss, a teacher, or even a family member. The most important thing is to be willing to learn and not afraid to receive feedback.

Here's another inspiring story: Here is Ratan Tata, one of the most respected industrialists in India, who often speaks about how J.R.D. Tata influenced his leadership style. J.R.D. instilled in him the importance of humility, long-term vision, and social responsibility. Ratan Tata's success isn't just a product of his intelligence but of the guidance he received and the discipline he exercised to follow it.

While mentoring involves external support, self-reflection is also equally as important. Ask yourself: What are my strengths? What are my weaknesses? Where do I see myself in five years? In ten years? These questions help you stay on the right track regarding your set goals and what to improve on.

Overcoming Obstacles

Discipline and goal-setting seem pretty straightforward, but life doesn't always work that way. There will be moments of doubt, distractions, and even failures. But remember, success isn't about avoiding setbacks; it's about persevering through them.

Use the example of the young entrepreneur who started a startup with big dreams: things went quite well initially, but then financial struggles hit his firm. Rather than giving up, seeking advice from mentors, reassessing his business model, and working tirelessly to turn things around, today his firm is a multi-crore success story.

In other words, this is the lesson: discipline will keep you going through the hard times, and goal setting keeps your mind on the bigger picture. It is easy to lose motivation when things do not go your way, but discipline tells you that you need to be anchored on why you started in the first place.

They are also prone to impulsive spending, believing that their income or savings can finance endless indulgences. As a matter of fact, it makes them grow in financial instability. Their approach to handling money tends to be disciplined. There's preparation for budgets and monitoring of expenses. Opportunities become investments that would benefit someone for some time.

Self-discipline is an elementary characteristic of developing good habits. It refers to doing things on purpose rather than just to satisfy short-term desires but instead working out for long-term goals. There are many forms of self-discipline: waking early, doing a fitness routine, having good nutrition, and not diverting oneself needlessly. Most people confuse discipline with constraint, and it is, actually, on the contrary, a liberator because of the fact that it gives them control over their impulses and decisions.

Self-control will then have to feature the living of a simple life. This doesn't automatically exclude comfort and luxury but rather focuses on what is most important. Simple living unshackles humans from being consumed by materialistic desires, freeing them to apply their time and energy to more meaningful ventures and activities. For instance, Mahatma Gandhi propounded a philosophy that made him a global influencer, yet he lived modestly, whose very simplicity he maintained could lead to deep personal impact and social influence.

This has modern examples, too, showing how simplicity is valuable. Well-known personalities like Warren Buffett are the richest but stay in modest houses, and he practices thriftiness. This isn't a coincidence; this is a habit formed as part of a disciplined mind wanting to attain sustainable living instead of superficial waste.

Role of Self-Awareness and Constant Learning

Actually, the heart of personal growth is self-awareness. This means an honest evaluation of strengths, weaknesses, and habits. One will realize patterns that have to change and even areas in which improvement is required. Writing a personal diary can help in the process as mentioned above. Recording daily thoughts and acts tends to bring about clarity on behaviours and why they are done.

For example, a manager might reflect on being a micromanager and realize that he or she micromanages because of the lack of trust between them and their team. As he becomes aware that this is so, then he can do a lot to foster more team-based execution where his team might handle the task themselves, which would improve team dynamics while also alleviating a load off the manager's shoulders.

Self-awareness comes from integrating training with self-awareness, which provides the ability to complete the job. The world moves forward at such speed that, without information, one would have no choice but to remain behind in this ever-changing, rapidly advancing world. Hence, academics should not be the only learning outcome; other forms include picking up a new skill, knowledge of diverse perspectives, or broad reading. Elon Musk is one prominent example of a successful individual. Musk-a partly self-taught, rocketry and coding extraordinaire- proves that this desire to learn can drive innovation and success.

Three Types of Habits: Personal, Practical, and Social

To build self-discipline and self-awareness, it would be beneficial to classify habits into three categories of habits:

1. Personal Habits: These are directly related to individual wellness. Examples include such things as exercise habits, healthy eating habits, and hygiene. Personal habits are the bedrock of a balanced life. Taking a disciplined approach to personal habits leads to the development of physical and mental resilience-otherwise known as coping skills when dealing with challenges.

2. Practical Habits: These are professional or work-related habits. On-time working, on-time completion of work, and effective management of time are concrete examples of practical habits that make one productive. A set time schedule which the entrepreneur maintains so as to avoid distractions will enable him or her to get more than what a procrastinator achieves.

3. Social Habits: They are related to association with society and social obligations. Paying taxes on time, obedience to traffic signals, and good behaviour towards others are some

illustrations. Social habits denote the esteem that a person feels for the greater social welfare. For example, complied norms of preserving the environment are not only a social obligation but also an exemplary expression of good living habits.

All habits must be evaluated. A person can have an exemplary personal habit, for example, exercising, while in another area, like social habits, she or he is lagging behind in doing the right thing about following laws. For holistic self-improvement, a person has to look at all the aspects of life.

The Influence of Role Models

The role models are major contributors in building habits. People like Ratan Tata, Sachin Tendulkar, and Lata Mangeshkar inspire millions in the way they remain disciplined, simple, and constant learners. They did not succeed solely due to talent but due to their never-ending efforts to perfect their habits.

Simple living is the power behind Ratan Tata's humility, despite his stature. Tendulkar's endless practice and focus without lapse represent self-discipline and produce desired fruits. One can learn a practical guide for good habits in the behaviour of such role models.

Building Good Habits

Building good habits is a slow process. It demands patience and consistency rather than a simple step to change. Here are some strategies for doing that:

- Start Small: One habit at a time. For example, if you want to wake up earlier, then begin by setting your alarm 15 minutes earlier than usual and work your way from there.
- Set Clear Goals: Define what you want to achieve. Goals give you direction and motivation. For example, you may not be saying, "I want to be healthy," but "I will exercise for 30 minutes every morning."
- Self-Reflection Practice: Always cultivate the habit of reflecting on your achievements and failures. Every day, write down your accomplishments on a note and analyze the mistakes you have committed on that day as well. This practice will keep you on track and make you familiarize yourself more.
- Surround yourself with inspiration. Read books by great leaders, watch motivational content, and interact with people who inspire you to grow.
- Consistency: New habits begin with some effort and time. Research indicates that adopting a new habit requires about three weeks to one month. Be consistent, even though you feel that things are moving at a slow pace.

- Self-Treatment: Reward yourself for the little you do. For instance, you could treat yourself to something you enjoy if you complete a week of following a new habit.

How to Change?

People change habits very hard. For instance, resistance to change, lack of motivation, or other distractions can be quite deeply ingrained as behaviours. But then, the application of discipline can be used to overcome such resistance. Examples abound in the following:

- If you easily get distracted and find it hard to focus on work, try the "Pomodoro Technique" and work with focused intervals lasting just a few minutes, then take a quick break.
- If procrastination is an issue, become better at breaking down actions into smaller, less intimidating pieces to reduce the potential overwhelm.

Creating a Life of Meaning

Finally, the purpose of self-discipline and self-awareness is to construct a life of purpose. A person who has discipline and knows about their values and goals is better prepared to face the world. The good habits adopted, the continuous learning process, and the action of being honest with oneself can make anyone's life a joyous and fulfilling experience.

It will be self-discipline and simplicity, anchored with self-awareness and a learning spirit, which will render life worth-living. It can be achieved by focusing on personal, practical, and social habits as well as drawing inspiration from great role models. Inner qualities are hard work, yet the rewards for such effort come in the forms of greater contributions to society and, above all, personal development and peace of mind.

The Future Road

These lessons will remind you to realize that habits do not automatically materialize overnight. They require patience, effort, and the willingness to try something for the first time. However, when these habits are rooted, they become like second nature, pushing you toward a successful and fulfilling life.

Start with one habit you'd like to either change or develop. It may be waking up an hour earlier, reading a book every month, saving a fixed percentage of your income-whatever you want, commit to it.

As Warren Buffett said, "Chains of habit are too light to be felt until they are too heavy to be broken." So choose your habits wisely-they're shaping your future every single day.

That's the end of part one of our series about the habits of rich people. Small, consistent acts pave the way to success-the rest is up to you.

Exercise:

Q1. Self-Reflection Exercise

Task: Reflect on your daily habits by answering the following questions:

1. What are the most common activities I engage in every day?
    - List your routine activities and categorize them as productive or passive.
2. How many hours per day do I spend on activities like reading, working, or learning?
    - Break down your day into blocks of time spent on various activities, focusing on the value they add to your life.
3. Which habits can I change or improve to be more disciplined and successful?
    - Identify one habit that, if improved, could significantly boost your productivity or personal growth.
4. How can I replace passive activities (e.g., watching TV, browsing social media) with more productive ones (e.g., reading, exercising)?

Follow-up:

- Write a commitment statement to adopt one new habit or improve an existing one for the next 30 days.

Q2. Goal-Setting Worksheet

Task: Break down your long-term goals into smaller, actionable steps.

1. Define your long-term goal.

  - Example: "I want to save ₹10 lakhs in 5 years."

____

____

2. Set a monthly goal.
   - Example: "I will save ₹10,000 each month."

____

____

3. List specific actions to achieve your goal.
   - Example: "I will cut back on unnecessary expenses and automatically transfer ₹10,000 to my savings account each month."

____

____

4. Track your progress.
   - Write down how you will monitor your progress (e.g., using a savings tracker, journal, or app).

____

____

Follow-up:

- Set a reminder to review and adjust your goals at the end of each month.

Chapter 7: The Way to Debt-Free Life

If a debt-free life is considered the hallmark of financial success, for many people, it remains something more of a dream. Debt sneaks into our lives through various channels, burdening our financial health and also future aspirations in the long run. From massive mortgage loans to small utility bills, every bill has a bit of a contribution towards our financial pathway. *Ek baar aap rin aur uske prakar samaj jaaye, fir aap apni zindangi mein paise sambhalna pakka se seekh jaoge.*

Types of Debt and Their Influence

Debt can be roughly categorized as essential and non-essential obligations. Essential debts include loans on homes, education, and vehicles—investments that often create assets or ensure future life chances. In contrast, non-essential debts involve discretionary spending such as loans for holidays, gadgets, or anything with a luxurious aftertaste. Even though one may find it inevitable to incur essential debt, non-essential debt can largely be controlled with sound financial discipline.

For instance, consider a young professional who recently moved to a metropolitan city like Mumbai. Renting a home may initially seem like the only viable option, but prolonged rental payments, when unchecked, can act as a recurring financial drain. Similarly, acquiring loans for non-urgent needs like a high-end smartphone may provide momentary satisfaction but contribute little to long-term financial well-being.

Debt effects go beyond monetary constraints. Financial liabilities that repeat can lead to emotional stress strain relationships and hamper the ability to pursue future aspirations. Effective debt management is therefore not a financial goal but a holistic enhancement of the quality of life.

Recognize All Forms of Debt

Debt seldom sits in the garage. Beyond loans and credit card dues, there exist understated forms, including:

- Recurring Obligations: Monthly rent, utilities, and school fees, though not classified as loans, constitute significant financial commitments.
- Unpaid Bills: Delayed payments for electricity, water, or other services can accrue penalties, exacerbating financial strain.
- Borrowed Sums: Informal borrowing from friends or family, while less formal than bank loans, is a debt nonetheless.

An understanding of the combined effect of such liabilities is essential. Each unpaid bill or late instalment adds to a financial lag that works against achieving the goal of being debt-free.

Debt Relief Solutions

Achieving a life free from debt requires conscious planning and constant action. *Yeh kuch cheeze aap kar sakte ho:*

- First, the habit of on-time bill and dues payment instils financial discipline. Not only will it help avoid penalties but also proper accountability.
- Prioritizing Loan Payments: Another area of loan repayment will be prioritizing loans with higher interest rates like credit cards or personal loans. By clearing these debts first, one can quickly decrease the compounding interest financial burden.
- Avoiding Non-Essential Loans: Not every dream is worth a loan. For example, one would argue that funding a child's education or buying a modest home may not always be justified, but buying loans for luxurious vacations or gadgets is avoidable. Financial decisions should be aligned with long-term stability rather than short-term gratification.
- Creating Emergency Fund: Saving at least six months of expense provides insurance during times of job loss or medical emergencies. This makes the use of loans much minimalized at times of crisis.

Financial Planning and Its Association with Debts

Financial planning is a guide that leads individuals toward a debt-free existence. An organized plan always integrates savings, disciplined spending, and very specific financial goals.

- Savings with a Purpose: Savings need not be an afterthought but a purposeful effort toward predetermined goals. Whether to meet emergencies, health necessities, or a child's education, savings towards specific goals add confidence in financial security.
- Budgeting as a Habit: Drawing up an annual financial budget will help one anticipate expenses and resource allocation. Budgeting is not about imposing restraints on spending but about ensuring every rupee spends leading to financial stability.
- Setting Financial Goals: Definite and Measurable Goals Give Direction. For example, aiming to pay off all debts before retirement or saving for a child's schooling abroad gives a definite goal in life. Goals need to balance immediate wants with long-term wants.

The Debt-to-Equity Ratio: What Businesses Can Learn

Businesses frequently use the debt-to-equity ratio to assess their financial health. This metric, if applied to personal finances, can offer valuable insights. A ratio of 1 or less signifies balanced financial health, while a higher ratio indicates excessive reliance on debt.

Consider an elderly person who is nearing retirement and has outstanding loans worth ₹2-2.5 million. Without planning, they might end up spending their post-retirement years due to debt repayment. Exactly as companies with heavy debt find it hard to raise money from financial institutions, similarly, liabilities of excess debt might make individuals face potential denial in future financial opportunities.

Developing Discipline for a Debt-Free Life

Debt management goes beyond financial literacy. *Aapko apni aadatein badalni hongi:*

- Self-Control: Instant gratification usually involves random spending. Rather, one should refrain and question whether or not the expense is necessary.
- Monitoring Expenses: The ease of transactions through digital payment products, such as Google Pay and Paytm, leaves one in danger of losing track of their expenses. Financial discipline will only be formed if proper monitoring of these spending habits is maintained.
- For High-interest loans: While one might need a loan to finance such huge investments as homes or education, it is important to try to negotiate favourable terms and clear dues on time. High-interest loans, if left unchecked, can snowball into a huge financial burden.
- Avoid Lifestyle Inflation: With increased incomes comes the expectation of a better lifestyle. However, expenses rising in tandem with incomes tend to offset the increases in real terms. The prudent investor manages a small expenditure budget even when his or her earnings are going up.

The Psychological Impact of Debt Freedom

Financial freedom is about not just the numbers; it's about peace of mind, and not having debt piling up on oneself. It allows for personal growth, investment in meaningful experiences, and securing future life for their loved ones. For many, the psychological benefits of being free from debts far outweigh any potential monetary savings, making this something important.

For instance, a middle-aged person cleared of debt could channel his hard-earned money into enriching his life; whether it may be in the form of hobbies, travel, or retirement planning. The feeling of accomplishment achieved through financial freedom is conducive to building self-confidence and stability.

Why One Should Have an Emergency Fund?

When I first heard about an emergency fund, it struck me as yet another requirement to which people with more money were committed. I felt it was something only financially savvy people did. I thought my monthly salary and a little savings here and there would get me through anything life threw at me. But life, as it does, taught me otherwise.

An emergency fund is not some fancy financial jargon-it's a safety net that can save you from the stress and uncertainty of unexpected expenses. Whether it's a sudden illness, an unforeseen job loss, or even something as simple as a broken refrigerator, these events always seem to arrive when we least expect them. With no emergency fund in place, these moments become financial disasters.

For instance, take my friend Ramesh. He was doing well, earning a decent salary and living a comfortable life in a big city. One day, his company downsized, and he was laid off. With no emergency fund to fall back on, he found himself struggling to pay rent and meet day-to-day expenses. He had to rely on his credit card for everything, which quickly turned into a mountain of debt. Had he set aside an emergency fund, things might have been different. Like most, I too had my wake-up call: my car broke down on the highway one evening, and the repair bill stood at a whopping ₹30,000. My entire savings went into that repair. This threw off my budget for months. Then it dawned on me how very urgent it was to really have a specific fund for emergencies. It's not just about being financially prepared; it is having peace of mind.

Imagine this: you have been saving for a family holiday for months. Suddenly, your child requires urgent medical treatment. Without an emergency fund, you are forced to use money meant for something enjoyable to cover something stressful. It is a lose-lose situation. With an emergency fund, however, you're able to step back in such situations because there's a buffer whereby you can handle it without disturbing your long-term plans.

Many of those think that they do not even earn enough to create an emergency fund. The same has always been true for me. However, I realized that every small, consistent saving accumulates to a lot over time. For example, if one saves ₹1,000 a month, this will add up to ₹12,000 at the end of the year. Of course, it isn't much at first, but it is a start.

We never expected to be financially affected during this pandemic.

My neighbour, Priya, had been a freelance designer. When the projects dried up, her only support was the emergency money she had in her savings account. She shared how she started saving small amounts of money years ago, even when her income was unreliable. That foresight allowed her to focus on finding new opportunities without the immediate stress of paying bills. Building an emergency fund isn't just about preparing for major crises. It can also cover smaller, everyday surprises. Last year, my washing machine broke down right in the middle of the monsoon season. Instead of panicking or borrowing money, I had it repaired using my emergency fund. The relief was priceless. Now, let's discuss how much you should save. Experts often state saving enough to cover three to six months' worth of expenses. For example, if your monthly expenses stand at ₹25,000, save at least ₹75,000 to ₹1,50,000. It may be a lot, but think of it like an Olympic race and not an individual sprint.
I started small. Every time I got paid, I would save 5% of my salary into my emergency fund. Some months were tougher than others, especially when unexpected expenses arose. But I stayed constant,

and it became a habit over time. Watching that fund grow gave me the accomplishment and security of knowing that I was ready for an emergency.

Making the mistake of placing one's emergency fund in an ordinary savings account is very common. This is my own past behaviour; I used it to finance some not-so-emergency needs. To avoid this temptation, I opened a separate account designated only for emergencies. It is still reachable when it is needed, but not so liquid that I would use it spur-of-the-moment.

Another lesson that I learned was that there is a need to review and adjust the fund over time. My wife and I got married and increased expenses. I found that my emergency fund isn't large enough anymore. So, I had to recalibrate and start saving more. Life changes you, and your emergency fund should change with it.

It's not just individuals who have to play this role; businesses use similar savings as buffers when a financial storm hits. A small restaurant near my house was saved during the lockdown because there was money saved by the owner for such occasions. It was not easy for him, but he kept his staff and business on their toes.

You also avoid taking high-interest loans from having an emergency fund.

My cousin Ravi was in a fix when his bike ran into trouble that needed urgent repair.

Without an emergency fund, he took out a personal loan. The loan covered the repair cost but the interest he had to pay was almost as much as the repair itself. It was a hard lesson for him and one that convinced me of the importance of saving for emergencies. Of course, there's great discipline involved in saving for an emergency fund. There are always strong temptations - an end-of-season sale, some fancy gadget, or a whim. I've been guilty of it all. But every time I resisted the urge, I kept telling myself that there was a bigger picture involved: namely, security in knowing I could handle the unexpected expense much more than temporary joy in buying something unnecessary. An emergency fund is about more than just the health of your financial situation; it's about emotional or mental well-being, too. Not knowing how you will pay for an unexpected expense can stress out your mental health. On the other hand, having a fund in place will give you confidence and peace of mind. If you wonder when to start, the answer is now. The sooner you start, the more time you will have to accumulate your funds. Do not look out for that high-paying job or expect a windfall. Start with what you have, no matter how little it may be. As they say, the best time to plant a tree was 20 years ago. The second-best time is today.

Most important, in hindsight, has been the emergency fund. This has been one of the finest financial decisions I have ever made. Not just a buffer against unexpected expenses, this is a foundation for a much more secure and less stressful life: from a small car repair to a major event, having that safety net has made all the difference.

So, take it from someone who's been there. Begin an emergency fund today. Your future self will thank you.

How to Create a Financial Plan with Specific Goals?

When I began planning my finances, it overwhelmed me. There were so many moving parts—savings, investments, debt, insurance, retirement planning, and so on. I didn't know where to start. Like many others, I thought that money would just magically work itself out if I kept earning and saving a little here and there. Over time, however, I learned that to gain much, it is necessary to have a clear financial plan which has defined objectives guiding me.

I do not know about you, but for me, having a financial plan was something alien when I first heard about it, but I soon discovered that without goals in place, I was just drifting. The financial plan is not merely tracking where your money goes. It's about setting specific and actionable goals and creating a roadmap to achieve them. And having clear objectives makes the journey far easier and less stressful.

The very first step when developing my financial plan was defining my objectives. This may seem mundane, but it took some time to really internalize what I wanted to obtain. My goals at first were pretty vague: "Save money" or "buy a house." However, such goals weren't specific and didn't provide a time frame. I realized I had to make them specific and more time-bound.

For instance, I didn't say, "I want to save money," but rather, "I want to save ₹2,00,000 in emergency funds by the end of next year." That changed the way I framed that goal; it seemed within reach, and I was able to formulate a plan for how I would get there. I broke down goals like "buying a house" into steps as well. My objective became: "I want to save ₹10,00,000 for a down payment on a house in the next five years."

At this point, I had no idea how much I had to save each month or even where to begin, but I knew my financial goals required timelines and metrics by which to judge my progress. So, I started to break the larger goal into smaller milestones. For example, to reach my target of an emergency fund of ₹2,00,000 by the end of the year, I have divided the whole sum into 12 months. This essentially meant saving ₹16,667 every month. Once I knew how much I needed to save, it was easier to identify what steps I would need to take towards that.

Next, I reviewed my income and expenses. I really had a good hard look at my budget and saw the areas for cuts. So, I started recording every small and big expense I was having- then discovered that many of the unnecessary expenses were what took me to restaurants and bought clothes that I hardly wear. Once I identified these unnecessary spending areas, I redirected that money toward my set goals. Cutting back wasn't easy, especially since it sometimes meant leaving behind little luxuries, but it was definitely worth it for what I saw in my savings account.

Let me explain using another example. My friend Neha also had that experience. She always used to talk about travelling the world, but whenever we caught up, she talked about how tight her finances were. But when I ask her what that financial plan looks like, she says she doesn't really have one. So, she's now decided to create a crisp objective: "I want to save ₹5,00,000 for a world trip in the next three years." She goes through the same process I described, breaking that down into manageable monthly savings targets. Neha started by saving ₹13,888 each month to meet her target. She tracked all her expenses and cut down on impulse purchases and unwanted subscriptions within two years. Thereby, she saved enough for her entire trip with financial freedom to explore her dream destinations.

Having outlined your objectives, it is time to build a strategy to meet them. For me, this involved deciding how I would allocate my savings. Some of the objectives needed urgent money, whereas others were for long-term saving, like retirement. It was at this point that I had to prioritize some of these goals. I would first focus on the creation of an emergency fund because a house was the next requirement. Retirement, however, took a back seat, though not absolutely, since a percentage of my income would go towards it.

Another aspect of the strategy I had to take into account was whether I wanted to invest my savings. On certain objectives, in fact almost those that I wished to achieve within the next short term, I favoured saving in low-risk, easily accessible accounts, such as fixed deposits or high-interest saving accounts. But for long-term goals, like retirement, I knew I needed to invest in mutual funds or stocks to grow my wealth. The key was balancing short-term safety with long-term growth potential.

As I started implementing my plan, I learned that flexibility is crucial. Sometimes things don't go according to plan. Life happens—there might be unexpected expenses, changes in income, or a shift in priorities. For example, I had planned to buy a car within two years. But when my parents fell seriously ill, I used that money to help fund their medical care, thereby setting back the timeline for myself. I didn't give up on my goal, but I adjusted the savings target and timeline. Having a flexible plan allowed me to pivot when needed and not feel discouraged.

Tracking progress is another important component of a financial plan. I made it a habit to review my plan every few months to see where I stood. This enabled me to change my savings goals if I found myself faring badly, or perhaps if I was pacing ahead of schedule, I could push myself to save more. Periodic reviews would keep me on my toes.

I learned another thing – putting smaller checkpoints into milestones to celebrate along the way. For example, once I had reached the middle point of my emergency fund goal, I rewarded myself by treating myself to a nice dinner. The small celebrations helped me stay motivated without losing sight of the bigger picture.

In summary, the process of crafting a financial plan with well-defined objectives involves understanding your goals, breaking them down into specific and measurable targets, and then creating a strategy to achieve them. It's not just a matter of saving money but making conscious intentions regarding where your money goes. By defining objectives and taking concrete steps toward them, you set yourself up for financial success.

Whether you're saving up for a dream vacation, a new home, or retirement, you'll find a clear financial plan that empowers you to take control of your future, one goal at a time. If you don't know where to start, just take that first step and begin by defining your goals and starting small. Eventually, you'll see how your plan really starts to pay off, and the sense of accomplishment will surely energize you to continue. And just like Neha and I, you'll be able to celebrate your financial successes and feel more secure about the future.

Exercise:

Q1. Multiple-Choice Questions (MCQs)

Q1: Which of the following is an example of essential debt?

a) Loan for a luxury vacation
b) Mortgage loan for buying a house
c) Loan for purchasing the latest smartphone
d) Loan for buying designer clothes

Q2: What is the first step towards achieving a debt-free life?

a) Taking a loan to consolidate all debts
b) Cutting down on discretionary expenses
c) Paying off loans with higher interest rates first
d) Ignoring debt until it becomes unmanageable

Q3: Which of the following is a recommended strategy for managing debt effectively?

a) Prioritize paying off low-interest loans first
b) Avoid setting financial goals
c) Pay bills and dues on time to avoid penalties
d) Increase credit card usage for better rewards

Q4: What is one psychological benefit of being debt-free?

a) Increased stress levels due to reduced spending
b) Freedom to invest in new luxuries
c) Improved peace of mind and personal growth
d) Difficulty in managing financial goals

Q2: Agree or Disagree?

Mark each statement as Agree or Disagree based on your understanding:

- Essential debts are always better than non-essential debts.
- Taking a loan for a high-end gadget is a good financial decision.
- Paying off high-interest loans first is a wise strategy.
- Budgeting is about restricting spending, not planning.

Q3. Quick Decision Test

What would you do in these situations? Choose the best option:

- You receive a bonus at work. Do you:
  a) Pay off a portion of your high-interest credit card debt?
  b) Splurge on a new gadget you've been eyeing?
- You are offered a loan for a luxury vacation. Do you:
  a) Take the loan and enjoy now?
  b) Decline the loan and save for the vacation?

Chapter 8: Personal Investment is the Need of the Hour

There is spending potential everywhere around us: from the irresistible cup of coffee at your favourite café to that latest gadget's release, money is spent not because one has to but because one can. For many, spending money has evolved into a need and even addiction; however, do we ever take a step back and consider whom we're giving our money to? Do we ask ourselves, "Am I investing this wisely, or could it be better invested for my future? " And if the answer is seldom or never, don't worry. You're not alone.

Most of us find ourselves entrenched in a consumerist mentality instead of an investor mentality. And the truth is, personal investment is no longer a choice but a necessity. We live in a world where silently, inflation eats away at the value of your hard-earned money. What you can buy with ₹100 today may cost you ₹150 or more in a few years. As such, the need to grow your money through investments has never been more urgent.

Chalo, shuru se samjate hai, investment kyu zaroori hai. Even with just limited income can make intelligent use of strategies in building a well-grounded financial future. *Aur ab yeh seekhni ki baari aapki hai!*

From Consumer to Investor: A Mindset Shift

In today's economy, everything is made to spend. Add to that the commercials, promotions, and discounts are not just marketing strategies but psychological nudges to get locked into a vicious cycle of consumption. I recall when I would see a sale and convince myself that I was "saving" money on something. However, what I did not know then is that every unnecessary purchase is a forgone investment that could be made on it and let it grow.

Becoming an investor takes a change in this mindset. Think about it: when you have spent ₹500 on a meal, it's all gone in a few hours. However, if that same ₹500 had been invested in a mutual fund or a fixed deposit, the same amount would have blossomed into a large sum of money over time. Shifting from spending to investing doesn't mean one stops enjoying life; instead, it is starting to invest one's financial future parallelly with the present.

Why Financial Literacy Matters?

One of the biggest barriers to investing is a lack of financial literacy. Unfortunately, many people in our country don't understand the basics of investing—what it is, why it's important, and how to start. I've met people who assume that investing is only for the wealthy or those who have a lot of extra money lying around. That couldn't be further from the truth.

Consider the story of my friend Ramesh, who is a school teacher with a modest income. For long, he thought he could not invest because of his income. Once he understood the basics of mutual funds and SIP, he began depositing just ₹1,000 a month. That small amount snowballed into something significant, and today, he has a very healthy investment portfolio that gives him full confidence about his future.

Ek aur baat yahan bahut zaroori hai - aapko paise invest karne ke liye bahut ameer hone ki zaroorat nahi hai. What you need is knowledge, patience, and willingness to start small.

Understanding Inflation and the Value of Money

One of the first lessons in financial literacy is understanding inflation. Suppose I invest ₹5 lakh in a life insurance policy today and it promises to give me ₹5 lakh after 15 years. It looks pretty okay at first glance. Have you considered what ₹5 lakh would amount to in 15 years? Your purchasing power could be really eroded, especially considering inflation. Today, ₹5 lakh could buy you a small car.

In 2037, it might just about cover a motorcycle.

It doesn't mean you should stay away from life insurance; it's a crucial part of financial planning. But this does highlight the importance of being informed as to the true value of your investments. When you make an investment, you need to think not merely about returns but also how those returns would stand up against inflation.

Diverse Investment Options

One believes that investing means 'investing all the money in one place' - like a fixed deposit or gold. These are good options, but not enough. In order to be genuinely successful in accumulating wealth, one needs to diversify their investments. Today, there are numerous avenues available, from stocks and mutual funds to government bonds and real estate. The key is to understand the pros and cons of each and choose appropriate options that align with one's financial goals.

Ek aur kahani sunati hu, meri ek dost ke baare mein. Voh apne saare paise ek regular savings account mein rakhti thi. She believed it was the safest way, but the very low interest rate wasn't keeping up with inflation for her money to grow rapidly enough. Once she learned about mutual funds and government bonds, she realized that these concepts provided better returns while remaining quite safe.

The 80:20 Investment Principle

An investment strategy that is simple yet powerful is the 80:20 rule, also known as the Pareto Principle. This principle may appear to be applied in myriad ways within everyday life or business, but applies wonderfully well towards personal finance.

The idea is this: 20% of your efforts should generate 80% of your results. In terms of investing, it means allocating a small portion of your income—let's say 20%—to investments that have the potential to deliver significant returns. The remaining 80% of your income can cover necessities and other expenses. This approach ensures that even if your income is modest, you're still making progress toward financial growth.

Let's take an example. Suppose you have ₹30,000 in your bank account every month. When applying the 80:20 rule, you could plan to save ₹6,000 for investments. You may plan to invest in safer options like fixed deposits and government bonds with ₹4,000, and ₹2,000 would go towards slightly riskier high returns from mutual fund investments. The same offers a path toward creating a huge wealth corridor as time passes.

The Pareto Principle also points out another important aspect of the financial plan: the identification and solving of the greatest impactful financial problems. The two most common are shock medical bills or sudden loss of a job; with strategic investing and an emergency fund, these can be minimized in their effects, and you can stay on track.

The Power of Starting Early

If there's anything I wish I had known earlier, it would be the importance of starting early. Indeed, small investments made consistently add up over time to significant accumulations through power-compounded returns. Compounding is essentially generating returns not only on an initial investment but also on returns on those returns. The earlier you start, the more time your money has to grow.

I'll share the story of my cousin Priya, who started investing ₹2,000 a month in a mutual fund at the age of 25. By the time she turned 40, her investments had grown to over ₹10 lakh. Compare that to her friend Ravi, who started investing the same amount at 35. At 40, Ravi's investments were worth only ₹3 lakh. *Par farak kya hai?* Priya had an extra 10 years of compounding working in her favour.

Taking Responsibility for Your Financial Future

At the end of the day, the responsibility for your financial future lies with you. While financial advisors and consultants can provide valuable guidance, it's crucial to have a basic understanding of your own investments. Blindly relying on others can lead to missed opportunities or even financial losses.

It's not just about securing your future; it's more about taking control of your life, and being prepared for whatever may come your way, be it the rising inflation or an unexpected emergency. It provides you with the freedom to live the life you want, free from the pressure of money worries at every step. So, if you haven't started investing yet, now is the time. Start small, educate yourself, and remember that every rupee you invest today is a step toward a brighter, more secure tomorrow. With a correct mindset and the right strategies, anyone, regardless of income, can be an investor who will be able to gain financial independence.

Types of investment with potential for long-run value creation

Investments in the long term are like planting a seed today and keeping it nourished to become a strong tree over time. Of course, there is a certain challenge attached to it; however, every small step is sure to count while making such investments. Significant milestones such as retirement, buying a home, or funding your child's education are just some ideal long-term investments. They also build security, stability, and the freedom to live your life on your own terms, not just make wealth.

Exploring Long-Term Investment Options

For long-term investments, it is crucial to understand the different avenues available. For example, equity mutual funds are one of the most popular routes. They offer the possibility of relatively higher returns over a period of 5-10 years and are managed by professionals, so much of the guesswork is taken care of. Equity funds enable you to own a small slice of many companies, thereby providing diversified investment opportunities against a single stock.

Consider the story of a family friend who started a SIP in an equity fund with a monthly investment of ₹2,000 ten years ago. The returns had far surpassed his wildest expectations, and he had even been able to pay for his daughter's higher studies abroad. It is not about the returns but the peace of mind that comes with knowing one has prepared for the future.

The Public Provident Fund is another long-term investment option that has a lock-in period of 15 years and tax benefits. It's excellent for risk-averse folks as the interest rate is revised quarterly but tends to stay above inflation. I opened my first PPF account at the start of my first job. For some time, it seemed too modest, but now it's one of the most dependable investments I have.

Role of Real Estate in Long-Term Investing

I personally also feel, real estate constitutes the foundation of long-term investment. Compared to stocks, it offers a tangible asset that in most cases appreciates with time. It is, however, expensive and requires proper research. The value of real estate is hugely dependent on location, infrastructure development, and future growth prospects.

I recall that my cousin bought a small flat on the outskirts of the city years ago when the area hadn't been developed. Today, that flat's worth has more than tripled in value due to the inflow of infrastructure projects. Real estate investments can be quite rewarding; however, they carry with them the requirement of patience because returns are hardly immediate.

Risk Management in Investment

Every investment does come with some amount of risk, and learning to manage this is essential. The best strategy for managing risk is diversification. Investment in a multitude of asset classes—equity, debt, gold, and real estate—will minimize the exposure to any particular sector.

For instance, during the 2020 pandemic, many stocks plummeted, but those with a diversified portfolio managed to cushion their losses with investments in gold or government bonds. It's a reminder that even in volatile times, a well-balanced investment strategy can protect your wealth.

Importance of Creating and Planning Investments

Investing without a plan is not unlike travelling somewhere without a map. You may indeed get to where you want to go, but it's a great way to be cranky. A good investment plan helps you chart your course, monitor your progress, and adjust accordingly as you go along.

One of the first steps in making a plan is identifying your objectives. Are you saving for a down payment on a house? Planning for your child's college fund? Each goal requires a different timeline, level of risk, and type of investment. For example, short-term goals like buying a car in three years might be better suited for a debt mutual fund, while long-term goals like retirement might benefit from equity-based funds or PPFs.

My financial goals were vague when I first began earning money. I saved irregularly without a specific purpose. It was only after consulting a financial planner that I understood the power of defining clear objectives. I then began allocating funds according to my goals, timelines, and risk appetite, and it transformed my view of money.

Creating a Budget to Support Your Investment Plan

A proper investment plan needs to begin with budgeting. Unless you know where your money is going, it is impossible to decide how much you can invest. I started by tracking my expenses using an app; it was an eye-opener in itself. I saw how much I was spending on discretionary items like dining out and online shopping. By cutting down on those, funds for investments were easily found without diminishing the essentials.

Evaluating Investment Options

Investment understanding is what also happens before getting into investment. Many people are put into fixed deposits (FDs) because of their apprehension of being safe. An FD provides safety but may not always beat inflation. If you have a 6% inflation and your FD is growing at 7%, then the real return is just 1%. This helps you make informed decisions.

Mutual funds have a higher risk, but then they also promise greater returns. Before investing in a mutual fund, read the scheme documents carefully, understand the risk factors, and see the past performance of that fund. Remember, past performances don't necessarily indicate future results. Yet, there will be light on how that fund has been managed.

The Role of Discipline and Consistency

Investing is not a one-time activity rather it needs to be a disciplined habit with a consistent approach. Compounding power reaps the best when investments are done frequently over an extended period of time. For example, investing ₹5,000 per month in a mutual fund with an annual return of 12% would amount to more than ₹23 lakh over 10 years. Take this forward for 20 years and one would earn nearly ₹1 crore. The sooner it is done, the better the benefit is reaped.

Adapting Your Plan Over Time

Life is full of uncertainties, and your investment plan must be flexible to accommodate changes. Loss of employment, birth, or a medical emergency may disrupt financial planning. Frequent evaluation of your portfolio with necessary adjustments ensures investment aligns with your goals.

I personally experienced this when I changed my profession and suffered a short-term reduction in income. I managed to remain on the right investment track, however, by reallocating parts of my portfolio and cutting back on discretionary expenses.

The Final Objective: Independence through Wealth

Ultimately, the purpose of investing is to achieve financial independence—the ability to live life on your terms without financial worries. Whether it's retiring early, starting your dream business, or travelling the world, financial independence provides the freedom to choose.

Investments are the bridge between your dreams and reality. By planning wisely, staying disciplined, and being patient, you can build a future that not only meets your needs but also fulfils your aspirations. Remember, every rupee you invest today is a step toward a brighter tomorrow.

Exercise:

Q1. Multiple-Choice Questions (MCQs)

1. Why is personal investment important in today's world?
    - A) It helps buy more consumer goods
    - B) It protects against inflation and helps grow wealth over time
    - C) It's a way to spend money on hobbies
    - D) It is a short-term strategy for earning money
2. Which of the following is NOT a typical long-term investment option?
    - A) Equity Mutual Funds
    - B) Fixed Deposits
    - C) Real Estate
    - D) Online Shopping
3. What is the 80:20 Investment Principle?
    - A) Spend 80% of income on luxury items and invest 20%
    - B) Invest 80% of your income in risky assets, and 20% in safe options
    - C) Allocate 20% of income to investments that yield high returns, and 80% to necessities
    - D) Invest 80% in gold and 20% in stocks
4. Which is an example of a risk-free investment with tax benefits?
    - A) Stocks
    - B) Real Estate

- C) Public Provident Fund (PPF)
- D) Mutual Funds

5. Which of these is NOT a step to successful financial investing?
   - A) Identifying your financial goals
   - B) Spending freely without planning
   - C) Diversifying your portfolio
   - D) Consistent monitoring and adjusting your investments

Q2: Agree or Disagree

Read the following statements and mark Agree (A) or Disagree (D).

1. Spending money is more satisfying than investing it for the future.
2. Inflation decreases the value of your money over time.
3. Personal investment requires you to be wealthy.
4. Starting small investments early can lead to significant financial growth.
5. Diversifying your investments helps reduce financial risk.

Chapter 9: The Role of Knowledge in Wealth Creation

Yeh toh sab hi ko pata hai, jahan Saraswati ji, vahan Lakshmi ji. It is not only a question of knowing numbers or account management; it is about cultivating a mindset, habits, and strategies for wealth creation. Although wealth creation might be a mysterious art, it finds its core in the most fundamental principle which is persistent learning. With an accelerating world at an unprecedented pace, lifelong learning is inevitable to win financially.

The Power of Emulating Success

One of the best ways to grow both personally and financially is to observe and emulate successful people. The rich have, throughout history, demonstrated habits and strategies that are replicable if studied carefully. Take, for instance, great entrepreneurs like Warren Buffett or Bill Gates. Their success is not accidental but the result of deliberate choices, disciplined actions, and a commitment to continuous learning.

When I was young, I would often wonder why only a few people in my community seemed to thrive financially while others struggled. Over time, I realized that those who succeeded weren't necessarily the most talented but the most curious and observant. They studied market trends, learned from their failures, and consistently surrounded themselves with people who inspired them. This underscores the importance of having a role model. Wealthy people do not stumble into money; they emulate others who have come before them.

But emulating does not mean comparison. Comparing ourselves to a role model may lead to self-doubt and unnecessary pressures. It is essential for us to remember that each person's journey may be unique. Bill Gates dropped out of college to pursue his vision, for example, but that doesn't have to be the case for anyone else. What one ought to emulate from him may be his lifelong learning practices, strategic thinking, or philanthropy while staying faithful to oneself.

Art of Giving and Wealth Creation

Another less-discussed yet very impactful aspect of wealth creation is giving. The concept that "giving increases wealth" may seem paradoxical, but it is based on spiritual and practical realities. Successful people and organizations do philanthropic activities. Corporate Social Responsibility (CSR) initiatives wherein companies set aside a portion of the profit for social welfare best represent this principle. Such practices not only contribute to society's betterment but also build up the reputation and influence of the giver.

Consider the case of Tata from India, which is well-recognized for its philanthropic activities. So, by investing in community development, education, and healthcare, it was capable of creating goodwill and loyalty to its stakeholders. On a personal level, even small acts of giving—donating to a local charity or mentoring someone—can create a sense of fulfilment and attract positive opportunities.

Entrepreneurial ecosystems in India have come to adopt this philosophy in the last few years. Business networks wherein people grow with one another have been on the rise. Such groups work based on mutual support: if you support other's success, they will help your success too. It brings about a cycle of growth and opportunity.

The Role of Visualization in Financial Success

Visualization is another powerful tool in the journey toward wealth creation. While most people dream of success, few take the time to vividly imagine themselves achieving it. Visualization isn't just wishful thinking—it's a mental rehearsal that aligns your actions with your goals.

Consider how exciting it feels to visualize yourself as a successful entrepreneur, running an organization and managing hundreds, as the leader. It both motivates you and readies your subconscious mind for all actions according to that vision. An athlete will vividly imagine themselves while performing or even before doing it because it enhances the performance level. Similarly, an entrepreneurial or professional personality can perform this activity so that his subconscious mind sets him toward success.

Another practice that pairs with visualization is waking up earlier to do some meditation or yoga. Meditation and yoga practices not only clear the mind but also enhance focus and creativity. The peacefulness of these early hours makes them an ideal space for setting intentions and visualizing your goals. Many YouTube videos and resources are readily available to guide people through the art of visualization and positive thinking.

Conscious and Subconscious Mind in Wealth Creation

It is crucial to understand how the conscious and subconscious mind interact to achieve financial success. The conscious mind deals with the process of decision-making, whereas the subconscious mind holds memory, habits, and emotions. Human beings live their lives mostly from the subconscious mind. *Basically, jo cheeze aapne apni puri zindagi mein seekha hai, aap zindagi bhar vahi amal karte hai.*

For instance, while working in an office, your conscious mind might focus on the task at hand, but your subconscious might wander to thoughts about a past failure or an unresolved issue. This division can hinder productivity and decision-making.

To succeed financially, it's essential to harness the power of your conscious mind while guiding the subconscious mind toward constructive thoughts. This requires discipline and awareness. Successful individuals are those who actively control their thoughts, focusing on the present moment and aligning their actions with their goals.

Consider the case of a young entrepreneur who faces a setback in their business. The subconscious may continue to think about it, but the conscious mind can shift its thoughts to solutions and opportunities. This conscious shifting of thoughts is the hallmark of resilience and success.

Discipline and the First Thought Principle

One important dimension to wealth creation is the capability of discipline and intentionality. It has been noticed that the very first thought in any situation, it mostly relates to our subconscious tendencies. If after a long week, you just sit and think, "I must sleep all day." Well, rest is good, but somebody who wants to be successful will think, "If I use today productively, then I will be one step closer to my goals.

This in no way means avoiding rest or leisure but rather learning to habituate towards actions which contribute to your goals. The rich tend to possess the ability to channel their energy towards what is worthwhile. They know that even the smallest action creates ripples in the grand scheme of things.

Never-stopping learning and financial literacy

Lifelong learning is the bedrock of financial success. In a fast-changing world, staying abreast of market trends, investment opportunities, and economic policies is non-negotiable. Financial literacy-the ability to understand and effectively use financial skills- is a critical component of this learning journey.

Take, for instance, the development of digital currencies and blockchain technology. Just a few years ago, the idea of cryptocurrency was a niche topic. Today, it has become a big deal in the global economy. A person who understood its potential in early times has enjoyed huge returns. Similar opportunities can be accessed in areas such as stock markets, mutual funds, and tax regulations by keeping abreast of them.

Knowledge as an Impetus for Growth

Ultimately, knowledge is the catalyst that transforms potential into reality. It equips individuals with the ability to make informed decisions, adapt to changing circumstances, and seize opportunities. The journey to financial success isn't linear—it's a dynamic process that requires curiosity, resilience, and a commitment to growth.

From here, wealth creation itself is just as much a matter of mindset as it is one of money. You become somebody similar to those who are successful by imitating, being of good service to others, utilizing the advantage of visualization, and embracing lifelong learning. *Samajhdari khud ek hathiyar nahi hai. Balki, voh asli takat ki chaabi hai.*

The Power of Knowledge: A Catalyst for Financial Success

Knowledge is an indispensable tool for anyone who wants to succeed and get wealthy. To the best of any profession, those who find their way to the top have mastered it, learn all the time, and adjust to changing conditions. When going about wealth creation, knowledge becomes not only helpful but indispensable. However, this is not about being formally educated but rather about knowing how to learn continuously and apply the learning strategically.

When we talk about success, financial literacy is very important; otherwise, one cannot create wealth. We talk about money, where to put it, and how to let it grow. Financial literacy is necessary in order to be equipped to evaluate opportunities and then make decisions, not losing into pitfalls that trap the uninformed. It is said that money attracts more money. What is behind the statement is the knowledge of how to make money work for you.

Take India as a case in point. The fields of biotechnology, artificial intelligence, and financial consulting are burgeoning with opportunities. These are areas where knowledge pays dividends, literally and figuratively. But to excel in those fields requires more than just a degree. It demands an understanding of the intricacies involved, the ability to predict trends, and, above all, a willingness to continue learning long after formal education has ended.

Nothing can be emphasized too much on the idea that knowledge is a lifelong pursuit. Being educated provides a foundation, but life changes so rapidly that any of us cannot just base our daily living on what we learned in school or in college. Learning has become a habit many of the world's successful and wealthy people do every day. They read much, network with other thought leaders, and participate in discussions meant to broaden their horizons. Knowledge is not just a tool for success but a lifestyle. The Timeless Nature of Knowledge

Unlike physical possessions, knowledge doesn't depreciate. Instead, it compounds, much like a well-planned financial investment. With the rapid advancement of technology, the accessibility of knowledge has never been greater. The internet provides a wealth of resources—courses, research papers, forums, and webinars—that can teach us about virtually any subject. The challenge lies not in acquiring knowledge but in having the discipline to seek it out and apply it effectively.

For instance, take the success stories of India's leading entrepreneurs. Their journeys are not just tales of hard work and determination. Rather, they also point towards the acquisition and application of knowledge. Whether it is about understanding market dynamics, consumer behavior, or technological trends, their success is built on a foundation of continuous learning.
However, there is a vast difference in the way people think of learning. While many may hold degrees, few have the eagerness to go beyond their formal education. Many cannot learn new skills or adjust to new technology. This is the greatest obstacle for many in a rapidly changing world. Literacy might be on the increase in India, but acquiring true knowledge-one that creates creativity and flexibility-still has a lot of mileage to go.

Interaction between Knowledge, Creativity, and Productivity

Creativity and productivity go well together with knowledge. Knowledge serves as the skeleton while creativity provides life to it and its application. Productivity is what helps to make this creative force effective. It is all together, these three factors that give way to success.

Creativity often thrives in the presence of knowledge. Imagine a writer writing a novel, an artist painting a masterpiece, or a designer conceptualizing a revolutionary product. In all these cases, knowledge provides the underlying structure—whether it is an understanding of literary techniques, the science of color and form, or the principles of engineering. However it is creativity that makes this knowledge meaningful and impactful.

Productivity ensures that creativity doesn't remain an abstract concept. It transforms ideas into actionable results. Successful people understand the importance of making the most of their time. They structure their days to allow for both creative exploration and the execution of those ideas. This balance is crucial, as focusing solely on one can lead to stagnation. Creativity without productivity is merely daydreaming, while productivity without creativity can lead to monotonous routines.

Time Management: A Way to Riches

Time management is perhaps the most underappreciated step toward wealth creation. Time, unlike money, cannot be made back once lost. It is a finite resource requiring thoughtful planning and intentional use. Rich and successful people master time usage. They know that every minute spent unproductively is a minute that might have been used to learn, create, or build something valuable.

It's quite clear that the more time, the greater financial success. People who succeed do what takes time. They can tell what's urgent from what's important, which they have to focus on in line with their overall goal. In a business setup, they give much time to doing research about the market, planning, and execution. And time for self-improvement since they know it's only their knowledge and expertise that would bring them there.

Conversely, most people end up trapped in short-term pleasures. For example, one can spend several hours on activities that provide short-term pleasure but no lasting value. Binge-watching, scrolling social media, or other passive pastimes eat away at what could have been used in a better way. Wealthy individuals, however, understand the cost of time: the alternative opportunity it has been wasted on.

Establishing a Knowledge-Based Daily Routine

The path to integrating knowledge, creativity, and productivity into your life begins with creating a routine. Consider maintaining a journal to track your daily activities, focusing on what you've learned or achieved each day. This habit fosters self-awareness and accountability, making it easier to identify areas where you can improve.

Reading is another habit that cannot be overstated. Most of the world's greatest minds give credit to their reading habits as the cause of their success. Warren Buffett spends hours each day reading books and newspapers, for knowledge is an investment with the highest returns for him.

Apart from reading, networking with people who know things can give you new opportunities and ideas. Creative and driven people inspire you to think differently and push your boundaries. In this way, your social circle is a valuable source of knowledge and motivation.

Knowledge into Wealth

To translate that knowledge into an ability to deliver financial success requires coupling it with actionable goals. This includes understanding the trend in markets and consumer needs versus emerging opportunities. For instance, digital marketing, artificial intelligence, and renewable energy are trendy today. By knowing the right things, you will be positioned to take advantage of these trends.

Financial literacy also plays a crucial role in the process. Knowing how to manage your finances and invest wisely will make sure that the wealth you create is sustainable. Knowledge without financial literacy is like building a house on sand-it lacks the foundation needed for longevity.

Creativity and productivity magnify the power of this knowledge. Whether one is launching a startup, writing a book, or designing a product, these qualities empower one to turn ideas into reality. Together with disciplined time management, they provide a foundation for success that can be sustained over a long period.

The journey to wealth creation is deeply intertwined with the pursuit of knowledge. It requires not just an understanding of your field but also the creativity to innovate, the productivity to execute, and the time management skills to balance it all. In an ever-changing world, those who commit to continuous learning and adapt their knowledge to current contexts are the ones who thrive.

Knowledge therefore needs to be a life-long friend. Be creative, and productive, and respect the time value you have in a relationship. That is when you fully tap into your own mind and open your doors to personal as well as financial growth.

Exercise:

Q1. Reflection: Personal Success Models

Think about someone you admire for their financial success. Answer the following:

- Who is this person?

____

- What habits or strategies do you believe contribute to their success?

____

____

____

- How could you incorporate one of these habits or strategies into your life?

____

____

Q2. Quick Reflection

Complete the sentence in your own words:

- A habit I can cultivate to enhance my financial success is ____ __________.

Q3: Visualization Practice

Close your eyes for a minute and imagine achieving one of your financial goals. Then, jot down three specific actions you could take to bring that vision closer to reality:

1. ______________________________

2. ______________________________

3. ______________________________

Chapter 10: Everyone Can Get Rich

In this book, we have explored the intricacies of money and the steps to achieving financial success. But at the heart of this journey lies an essential question: "What do I truly want in life?" It is not enough to harbour vague dreams of riches or success; one must pinpoint specific aspirations and commit wholeheartedly to pursuing them. This clarity of purpose, coupled with determined effort, paves the way to success.

We all dream of being big, successful, and financially affluent. However, dreams sans workable plans remain just dreams. Real change happens once those aspirations are chiselled out to become specific and achievable targets. To desire wealth comes easily, but to track it requires focus. Ask not just if you want success but in what field and how. *In fact, yahi asli tareeka hai, safalta ke beej bone ka.*

Imagine the following: "I want to be a successful engineer and earn a lot of money." Such a declaration sounds ambitious, but it lacks any clarity. Success in engineering or any other field is purely through choices: What branch of engineering? Civil, mechanical, software, or electronics? Which avenues within that branch will have the best opportunities? Should one target a government position, a private sector role, or a venture into entrepreneurship? All these questions will take reflection. For instance, a software engineer may start out considering it to be an overly lucrative field, but one's potential success depends on what kind of industries they specialize in, and the companies one decides to work with; they all have to keep up in this lightning-fast world of changing tech landscapes. Every field has a potential to it, but not everybody maximizes it.

Creating Your Definition of Rich End

Being "rich" is subjective. It could mean a luxurious home for some and financial independence or the means to travel the world for others. However, material possessions cannot define wealth. A person who owns a debt-free home but has no steady income feels secure in one aspect but vulnerable in another. He will feel the pleasure of richness and enjoy being in such an illusionary world but will lack the financial stability in his life. True wealth is the balancing act. It's not about the wealth you earn, but rather the freedom and security and the opportunities your money opens for you.

To get wealthy, you must first determine what wealth is to you. Is it about a certain lifestyle, the ability to provide for loved ones, or the freedom to explore passions without worrying about money? Once you define what "a lot of money" means in your context, you can create a roadmap to achieve it. **Setting Financial Goals with Purpose** Goals are the compass that directs your financial journey. Without clear, actionable objectives, even the most ambitious individuals can lose their way. When setting goals, think beyond vague aspirations like "earning more money." Instead, envision specific milestones: saving a certain amount by a given age, investing in property, or building a thriving business. Let's revisit the example of an engineer. It is not enough to aspire to become a software engineer; one must also consider the specific routes within that profession. Which programming languages or platforms are in high demand? Should they focus on AI, cloud computing, or cybersecurity? Every choice should be made with a long-term vision of success.

Similarly, how much you want to earn may be broken down into achievable steps. If your ultimate goal is to have a net worth of ₹5 crores at the age of 40, calculate how much you need to save, invest, or earn annually to reach that target. The big picture can always be broken down into small parts and tackled systematically.

Alignment of Goals with Financial Planning

Financial planning fills the gap between dreams and reality. It requires clear knowledge of your current resources, available opportunities, and potential risks. Begin by reviewing your income, expenses, and savings. What areas can you cut back on to free up more for investment? How can you diversify your sources of income so that you can have steady finances even in times of uncertainty?

Investments are key to the construction of wealth. This is whether in stocks, real estate, mutual funds, or your own business; each investment should be working in tandem with your long-term financial goals. However, it is dangerous to invest blindly. Prepare yourself by being equipped with the tools and knowledge to make informed decisions. The financial world is intricate. Concepts such as inflation, interest rates, and market trends, among others, can arm you with the necessary information to negotiate its complexities.

Consistency is King

Consistent effort works toward the goal. One of the primary reasons for failure is that many people get impatient and seek overnight gains. The money you will acquire does not come overnight but over time. Regardless of whether one is building a career running a business or investing in the stock market, the bottom line remains: stay persistent and allow the strategies the time to show their results. *Voh khete hai na, bas karm karte jao, fal ki chinta mat karo.*

Successful people understand that time is money. They treat every day as a chance to move closer to their goals. Whether through acquiring new skills, widening their professional network, or exploring innovative ideas, they ensure that their efforts are never stagnant. If you commit even one hour of your day to activities that work towards your financial goals, you will be surprised at how much you can achieve in months and years.

Believing in Your Potential

This is believing that you are capable of achieving financial success. Many people limit themselves due to their inability to believe in themselves, or by doubting the dreams they have. It's not that the money has been made for a privileged few; it is open to anyone willing to work for it. However, this must go with action.

Seek an atmosphere of challenge and inspiration: have mentors and workshops, a continuous learner. The earth is rich in resources when discovered. When you invest much in the growth of such experiences with which you seek, the bigger your return will be through either education or relationships.

The journey to wealth is not just a matter of strategy but of mind as well. Build a growth mindset, and challenge life with an adaptable nature. As the world evolves faster each day, one is left with no choice but to evolve to the best and get open to change, and sometimes one finds out that it takes a setback to propel toward greatness.

Everyone can be rich. It's not just about the money, but also the life one lives with abundance, fulfillment, and purpose. It is all about clear goals, thoughtful planning, and unwavering determination toward financial success. Remember, the journey may be long, but the destination is worth every effort. Believe in yourself, stay focused, and take the first step today.

Each individual has his or her unique aspirations and goals, and no profession or field is too small to aspire to succeed. What differentiates those who succeed from those who just exist is the way of doing things-from daily practices, envisioning success, and remaining focused on one's goals. The story of modern companies such as Byju's and Unacademy epitomizes how ambition, purpose, hard work, and meticulous planning can turn a vision into a multi-billion-dollar reality. Behind every success lies clarity of purpose and daily effort traits that anyone could adapt to fulfil their own financial dreams.

Thinking about wealth is not sufficient to become wealthy; action is what serves as a bridge between dreams and reality. People say, "I want to be rich," but without concreteness in a plan, these aspirations become mere wishes. First, define your relationship with money: To you, what is the meaning of wealth? Is it owning a home, building a business, travelling the world, or just living debt-free? Clarity helps channel energy in the right direction, turning ambiguous desires into actionable goals.

The power of positive thinking and visualization is important in this journey. Visualization is not merely daydreaming; it is actually planning the life you desire. Imagine yourself sitting in that promotion seat, running a successful business, or reaching the financial goals you set. All this trains your mind by emphasizing your goal and making it view more opportunities for that goal. Then, positive thinking fuels that resilience. Obstacles will eventually present themselves, but a solution-oriented mindset keeps the drive alive.

Writing down your goals each day is as simple as it is powerful to cement commitment. This act takes vague thoughts and turns them into concrete declarations, reminding you daily of what you are working toward. Consider a young attorney who aims to become one of the senior partners at a respected firm in five years. Each morning, it could be, "I will be a senior partner by 2029, earning seven figures and leading landmark cases." This habit builds discipline, so the daily activity becomes more readily aligned with the long-term goal.

Disciplined routines accompany daily practices like goal writing. Start each day with an intentional act that moves you closer to your ambitions. For some, this may mean dedicating the first hour of the day to learning new skills, for others, perhaps to networking or working on a business strategy. Whatever the daily activity, it becomes an earnest process that leads to small, consistent steps that eventually sum up to exponential results. Illustrative example: take doubling income; it can start with mastering new skills or searching for different incomes. Such disciplined effort, over months and years, can add significant growth to one's finances.

The second most important is tracking progress and celebrating small wins. Financial success is a marathon, not a sprint, and recognizing incremental achievements keeps one motivated. If you're saving up to the tune of ₹10 lakhs, celebrate reaching every ₹1 lakh milestone. These acts of celebration reinforce your capacity to achieve greater feats for this long haul.

Belief in yourself is the cornerstone for wealth creation. There are numerous incidences in the history books of people who started with little and made it big through their unshakable belief and relentless efforts. Think of Dhirubhai Ambani, starting as a petty trader and building one of India's largest conglomerates. His story is a testifying idea that wealth creation is not always a matter of outer circumstances but about inner conviction and perseverance.

Time management is another essential aspect of daily discipline. Everybody has the same 24 hours, but how those hours are utilized makes the difference between stagnation and success. Keep only activities that contribute directly to your financial goals, and not those distracting activities. For example, an upcoming entrepreneur may spend their evenings doing research on the marketplace or designing their products instead of wasting their evenings scrolling mindlessly on social media. These focused efforts compound over time, bringing you closer to your aspirations.

Visualization and positive affirmations can be particularly powerful when combined. Start each day by picturing the life you want to lead—be it a luxurious home, financial independence, or the ability to support causes close to your heart. Follow this with affirmations that reinforce your belief in achieving these goals. Even statements like "I am capable of creating wealth" or "Every day, I am closer to financial freedom" can change your perspective from one of doubt to one of determination. The subconscious mind, if exposed repeatedly to such affirmations, will eventually begin to accept them as reality and guide actions into sync with your vision.

Financial discipline also contributes to the realization of dreams. While making more money is one aspect of the equation, managing it is as important as making it. Develop saving habits like saving a certain percentage of your income, investing in a wise manner, and avoiding unnecessary expenses. These will not only secure the present but lay down the building blocks for the future. A daily review of your finances, helping you track your expenses, monitor your investments, and update your budgets keeps you in control and aligned with your goals.

Surround yourselves with people who can inspire and motivate you. The company you keep will greatly affect your mindset. Engage with mentors, colleagues, or friends who may inspire you with the same vision of success or new ideas that may encourage you. A support system will be your safety net during the tough times and a sounding board for new ideas to feed into your journey towards wealth.

Daily practices should also encompass gratitude and generosity. While working towards gaining wealth, it is important to thank God for the journey so far and for the resources you have already acquired. Gratitude ensures happiness keeps you humble and gives you pause, lest the pursuit of the purse turn into an empty exercise. And sharing your good fortune with other people finds a sense of satisfaction beyond your money.

In essence, the path to wealth is personal, defined by what you want, choices made, and efforts applied. The synergy of daily practice, visualization, and thinking positively propels one to their goals. Each new day brings a chance closer to the life envisioned. Consistent effort prevents all opportunities from being lost.

In summary, financial affluence is not the prerogative of a select few; it is only for those who will take dedication and commitment to achieve their goal, working through daily disciplines and remaining optimistic. Wealth is not just money, it stands out as an instance of resilience, creativity, and the ability to dream big. By fostering these attributes and diligently practising them every day, one can translate his dreams into action. Believe in your potential, take consistent action, and watch as your life evolves into the success story you've always imagined.

Exercise:

Q1: Break Down the Big Picture

Write down one big financial goal you have (e.g., "Save ₹1 crore by age 40").

____

____

Now, break it into smaller steps:

Annual Target: _________________

Monthly Target: ________________

Weekly Action: _________________

Q2: Financial SWOT Analysis

Complete the following:

1. Strengths: One thing I'm already good at financially is _____________________.
2. Weaknesses: One area I need to improve is ______________________________.
3. Opportunities: One opportunity I can take advantage of is _________________.
4. Threats: One potential risk to my finances is ____________________________.

Answers:

Chapter 3

Q1: Multiple-Choice Questions (MCQs)

1. b) Reducing the purchasing power of money
2. b) House you own
3. b) It increases the cost of living, requiring adjustments in your budget
4. b) Loan repayment should be no more than 25-30% of your monthly income.
5. b) Combining multiple loans into one loan at a lower interest rate

Q2:

- Assets: Stocks, Business you run, Rental property generating income, Personal savings account
- Liabilities: Home loan, Car loan, Credit card debt, Furniture and appliances (if depreciating)

Chapter 5:

Q1. Multiple Choice Questions (MCQs)

1. b) Following internal commitments to personal goals

2. b) External discipline is imposed by others, while self-discipline is internal and self-motivated.

3. c) Elon Musk
4. c) Long-term success requires time, effort, and patience.

Chapter 7:

Q1:

1. b) Mortgage loan for buying a house
2. b) Cutting down on discretionary expenses
3. c) Pay bills and dues on time to avoid penalties
4. c) Improved peace of mind and personal growth

Chapter 8:

Q1:

1) b) It protects against inflation and helps grow wealth over time
2) d) Online Shopping
3) c) Allocate 20% of income to investments that yield high returns, and 80% to necessities
4) c) Real Estates
5) b) Spending freely without planning

Verses Kindler Publication

Reach us through our website -
https://www.verseskindlerpublication.com/
For more information visit our Instagram or Facebook page.

www.ingramcontent.com/pod-product-compliance
Lightning Source LLC
Chambersburg PA
CBHW041302210926
51847CB00010B/113
* 9 7 8 9 3 5 6 0 5 4 8 8 2 *